THE OFFICE OF THE PROPHET
(Second Edition)

THE OFFICE OF THE PROPHET
(second edition)

By
Apostle Leslie D. Richardson

TATE PUBLISHING
AND ENTERPRISES, LLC

The Office of the Prophet
Copyright © 2013 by Apostle Leslie D. Richardson. All rights reserved.

No part of this publication may be reproduced, stored in a retrieval system or transmitted in any way by any means, electronic, mechanical, photocopy, recording or otherwise without the prior permission of the author except as provided by USA copyright law.

The opinions expressed by the author are not necessarily those of Tate Publishing, LLC.

Published by Tate Publishing & Enterprises, LLC
127 E. Trade Center Terrace | Mustang, Oklahoma 73064 USA
1.888.361.9473 | www.tatepublishing.com

Tate Publishing is committed to excellence in the publishing industry. The company reflects the philosophy established by the founders, based on Psalm 68:11,
"The Lord gave the word and great was the company of those who published it."

Book design copyright © 2013 by Tate Publishing, LLC. All rights reserved.

Published in the United States of America

ISBN: 978-1-62994-804-1
1. Religion/Prophecy
2. Religion/Christian Education/General
13.10.04

THE OFFICE OF THE PROPHET

TABLE OF CONTENTS

FOREWORD	iv
ACKNOWLEDGEMENTS	vi
PREFACE The Office Of The Prophet – In Alignment With Apostolic Order	ix
CHAPTER 1 The Testimony Of Jesus Christ	1
CHAPTER 2 The Origin Of The Office Of The Prophet	14
CHAPTER 3 The Audience Of The Prophet	30

Table of Contents
The Office of the Prophet

CHAPTER 4
Locating The Prophetic Voice — 47

CHAPTER 5
How To Know If You Are Called
To The Office Of The Prophet — 67

CHAPTER 6
How To Develop This Gift — 104

CHAPTER 7
How To Protect This Gift — 128

CHAPTER 8
How To Carry This Gift — 148

CHAPTER 9
How To Serve In The Local
House — 171

♦ ♦ ♦

Table of Contents
The Office of the Prophet

CHAPTER 10
How To Serve In Governmental Affairs … 185

CHAPTER 11
How To See Into The Spirit World … 203

CHAPTER 12
The Gift Of Discernment Working In The Prophet … 222

AFTERWORD TO THE PROPHET … 235

♦ ♦ ♦

THE OFFICE OF THE PROPHET

♦ ♦ ♦

FOREWORD

This book, "The Office of the Prophet," by Apostle Leslie D. Richardson, is an inspired document in due season. The timing of such a treatise is immeasurable in its importance to the Body of Christ. The information provided is for "such a time as this," to help all of us to be better prepared for the soon coming of our Lord and Savior Jesus Christ for His church.

Since the end times speak to us of an increase in the number of "false" prophets, it is incumbent upon us to "know and recognize" the true prophets of God. The information presented in the book does an excellent job of enabling us to ascertain truths on this subject. The author is to be commended for his research and commitment. I highly recommend this book for your prayerful consideration. I know the

♦ ♦ ♦

Foreword
The Office of the Prophet

author to be a truly dedicated and sincere man of God.

It has certainly been both a pleasure and privilege to have mentored the author of this great work. I am grateful to God for whatever degree of influence I may have had on his life and his spiritual development. To God be the glory! May God continue to bless and prosper him in all of his endeavors.

In his service to the Body of Christ,
Bishop Earl O. Holiman
Pastor of Bethsaida Temple Christian Center, Denver, Colorado

♦ ♦ ♦

THE OFFICE OF THE PROPHET

♦ ♦ ♦

ACKNOWLEDGEMENTS

I dedicate this project to my Heavenly Father for downloading into my heart this precious revelation and trusting me with the responsibility to convey its importance to the church.

Honor to Pastor Lily Ray Richardson, my beloved wife, for your strength and encouragement while laboring with me in the trenches of ministry. Your dedication and support means everything.

Special thank you to our awesome children and grandchildren: Leslie II (Lynette), Marcus (Karla), Jasmine, Joshua, Leslie III, Laila, Adriel, and Mya.

Without Deacon O.J. Richardson, my father and first published author in our family, this project would not be possible.

♦ ♦ ♦

Acknowledgements
The Office of the Prophet

Dad, your book entitled, "Nimrod the Mighty Hunter" is exceptional.

A tribute to my beautiful and anointed mother Pastor Geraldine Richardson—Thank you mom for being my very best friend and for always being by my side to cheer me on. I thank God for you and dad for being so supportive of all that I do and, more importantly, for sharing the love of Jesus Christ with me and teaching me how to serve Christ with a heart of integrity. Thank you Mom!

Tymesha Edwards, my spiritual daughter, thank you for your persistence in encouraging me to publish this book.

To each member of My Father's House Christian International Discipleship Center, I would like to say thank you to the number one congregation on the planet! You are the very best congregation and without

♦ ♦ ♦

Acknowledgements
The Office of the Prophet

your faithful support throughout the years, this book would not have been possible.

Finally, thank you Pamela Gilmore for the tremendous job in editing this project and for the unsurpassed level of excellence you brought to the project.

~

THE OFFICE OF THE PROPHET

♦ ♦ ♦

PREFACE

*The Office Of The Prophet
In Alignment With Apostolic
Order*

I have written this book to share what the Lord has given me concerning ***the office of the prophet*** and to activate the prophetic in the lives of those who read it. My hope is that this specific God-given revelation concerning the office of the prophet will stir the Body of Christ to align itself with fivefold power and dominion and recognize that the office of the prophet indeed is in proper alignment with apostolic order.

The lack of comprehensive teaching and erroneous doctrine concerning the fivefold ministry, has caused the body of Christ to come out of alignment with apostolic and prophetic ministry. I believe

♦ ♦ ♦

Preface
The Office of the Prophet

that while the body of Christ has received the foundational truth of this doctrine, it has become stuck and does not fully understand what the Apostle Paul was trying to impart in **Ephesians 4:13:** ***Till we all come in the unity of the faith, and of the knowledge of the Son of God, unto a perfect man, unto the measure of the stature of the fulness of Christ:***"[1]

W.E. Vine defines the apostle as "one sent by God."[2] God never sends an apostle without a prophetic word. I know this is controversial theology for many because of the adoption of the old wineskin teachings that is referred to as fivefold

---

[1] Unless otherwise noted, all scripture references contained herein are from the 1769 Oxford King James Bible Authorized Version (KJV). (Bold/Italics added for emphasis.)

[2] Vine, W.E. *Vine's Expository Dictionary of New Testament Words*, Peabody Massachusetts (1989). Unabridged Edition.

Preface
The Office of the Prophet

ministry.³ Edward Irving,⁴ a theologian and Presbyterian pastor who in 1824 established The New Apostolic Movement, was a strong proponent of the teaching of the fivefold ministry. Irving submitted to revelation concerning the operation of the gifts that are given to the church by Christ. Many of his colleagues refused to embrace his teaching and he was thereby met with great opposition. Others however did embrace the perpetuity of the offices of the fivefold ministry. In 1948, the Latter Rain Movement was introduced to the body of Christ. And in the early 1980s, Apostle Charles Peter Wagner also began to teach the doctrine of the fivefold ministry and was the author of

---

³ My reference to the old wineskins teaching refers to Jesus' parable in *St. Luke 5:36-39* when Jesus was criticized and rejected by the Scribes and Pharisees because they wanted to preserve their traditions. The old wineskins represent Judaism and the Law while the new wine symbolizes grace.

⁴ Next Reformation: *New Apostolic Reformation 3*. Retrieved from http://nextreformation.com/?p=865.

♦ ♦ ♦

Preface
The Office of the Prophet

The New Apostolic Churches.[5] It is my belief that God preordained these men of God to preserve the importance of the fivefold ministry in the body of Christ.

I want to emphatically convey the need of having a clear understanding that this spiritual operation in the body of Christ is critical and has always has been a part of God's plan to bring heaven to earth. If the body of Christ is to be prepared for the return its King, Jesus Christ, then the inclusion of apostolic and prophetic ministry must be embraced by the bride.[6] The Apostle Paul understood that this was the intended goal for the body of Christ.

Because I am called to "disciple" the Body of Christ and not merely to produce

---

[5] C. Peter Wagner, Wikipedia. Retrieved from http://en.wikipedia.org/wiki/C._Peter_Wagner.

[6] Revelation 2:17

Preface
The Office of the Prophet

"church members," it is imperative that I facilitate this revelation concerning the office of the prophet in a way that encourages, inspires and equips the prophet for Kingdom work. I am positive that the Lord Jesus Christ will give me additional revelation concerning the office of the prophet, and when He does, I will publish another book.

As I am sure many others have, I have asked this question many times: "Should I write a book on this subject?" After many years of questioning, "**THE OFFICE OF THE PROPHET**" has finally become a written reality!

As far back as I can remember, there has been a sense of supernatural awareness in my life, although in my early years, I did not know what "it" was. Naturally, like many others who grow up with religious consciousness, that awareness shaped my

♦ ♦ ♦

Preface
The Office of the Prophet

thoughts and attitudes concerning the questions of life.

I grew up in a Christian home and I remember my mother gathering all of her children and taking us to church. Occasionally, she would even talk my dad into going. Of course, as children, our only thoughts were how to survive service this Sunday—we knew we would be there for a long time!

I was raised in the small town of Lansing, Michigan during the late-sixties and early-seventies, at a time when drugs were prevalent and "loose living" was the norm. You see, because of my upbringing and social environment, the proverbial thought was that I would either be dead or in prison by the time I reached the age of 21.

After turning eighteen, I enrolled in an alternative education program and began

Preface
The Office of the Prophet

working on completing my studies to receive a high school diploma. While there I was introduced to a school counselor, Jack Porter. It was through this young man that I began to gain self-confidence and to believe that I had something of value and of significance to offer the world. Jack began to teach me the boundaries of life and I respected him for that.

In April, 1975, I enrolled in a typing class but wanted to drop the class because the teacher was "grossing me out." I spoke to Jack and while in his office, he asked if I was interested in Karate. I responded with an overwhelming "yes!" I emphatically told him that I already knew a little bit about Karate because after all, I watched the television show "Kung-Fu" with David Carradine! He just smiled and invited me to class. I will never forget my first day! I knew that I had found my place and I stopped smoking cigarettes that day! Jack

♦ ♦ ♦

Preface
The Office of the Prophet

and I began an awesome journey; he took me under his wings and introduced me to the Michigan State Karate Club. It was through that experience that I learned self-value and self-respect; I also learned how to respect others. Nineteen months and several championship trophies later, I received my First Degree Black Belt.

After moving to Denver, Colorado in 1977, I began to recognize that there were many areas of life I yet had to learn. With the confidence and boldness of life, I struck out to experience everything that I could to find my place in this world. Looking back over my life, I recall several instances that I now call "God Moments"—moments when destiny and faith meet and a decision is made that begins to chart our lives.

Because I was exposed to the philosophy of martial arts, it was natural for me to become interested in eastern religions

♦ ♦ ♦

Preface
The Office of the Prophet

such as Taoism and Buddhism, as well as in Transcendental Meditation. Each one of these disciplines seemed to add something of value to my humanity; however, they never completely filled the internal void aching to be satisfied.

It was not until August 1982, that I truly heard the gospel of Jesus Christ. Another mentor (now one of my closest friends) who happens to be the Bishop of Bethsaida Temple Worship Center in Denver, Colorado, Bishop Earl O. Holiman, was the first person to inspire me to make a decision to accept Jesus Christ and receive Him into my life. At the time, I did not fully understand what I was doing, but there was something about the manner in which Bishop Holiman delivered the gospel message of Jesus Christ that inspired me to say yes, yes, yes!

♦ ♦ ♦

Preface
The Office of the Prophet

Because of the discipline received from martial arts, I understood the need to discipline myself in the word of God if I was going to get better. I began attending Bible studies in the homes of various members. During one of these Bible studies I had an extremely embarrassing moment. We were all asked to read out loud, but because I was not confident in my reading skills, when it was my time to read I completely froze. I made up an excuse and did not read. The truth is that I was functionally illiterate. For years I was able to simply get by with reading at about a third grade level. This moment caused a tremendous setback in my Christian development. After discovering that I was not the best reader in the group, I began to believe that I provided no value to the group. No one guided me through that experience or helped me and consequently, I returned to the world I had left behind.

♦ ♦ ♦

Preface
The Office of the Prophet

But I missed my newfound faith in Jesus Christ, and God in His sovereignty, was still leading and directing my life. As an aspiring martial artist and model, I began filming local commercials as well as doing print work with companies in Denver. A friend introduced me to Donald Todd, a vocal coach in theater. Donald was a wonderful man and I believe it was through this relationship (another God Moment) that I was forced to face my fears about reading in public. Bwana (Swahili for "Sir") Todd forced me to stand in front of him, to speak to him, and to articulate my words. He also forced me to read out loud, an exercise that developed my reading skills and helped to boost my confidence. I must confess that I continued to struggle with reading out loud because I had not yet dealt with the soul wounds of embarrassment.

One day I decided to take my son, Leslie II, to the church of a friend of ours

♦ ♦ ♦

Preface
The Office of the Prophet

who kept bugging me to come. At this service on October 15, 1989, my life was forever changed! Pastor Larry Washington was teaching from Ephesians 6 and his subject was, "Putting On The Whole Armor Of God." Again, because of my background in martial arts, the sermon resonated and hit home with me; I found myself at the altar weeping. Understand that it was not my nature to weep—ever! After all, by then I had earned a Fourth Degree Black Belt and my philosophy was that real men do not cry! I explained to Pastor Washington how I had tried this before and that I needed the power of the Holy Ghost to help me. He gave me a little book by Dr. Frederick K. C. Price entitled, "Holy Spirit: The Help We Need." He also instructed me to read the book of Proverbs.

The next morning after work at about one o'clock, I was sitting at my kitchen table reading the first seven chapters of Proverbs.

♦ ♦ ♦

Preface
The Office of the Prophet

Suddenly I was able to read with the confidence and boldness that only God could have inspired! I opened my mouth and began to read out loud and by the time I got to the seventh chapter of Proverbs, I was caught up in the Spirit and began speaking in tongues! I had never before experienced speaking in tongues! Through that experience I recognized that the supernatural power of God was not only real, but that His power was available to me and, as a matter of fact, was working in me! Since that day I have not looked back.

I returned to my pastor, Bishop Holiman, and sat at his feet in a position of learning. There the Lord spoke a word to me, "Launch out and plant a church in Denver." By that time I was an associate elder and minister at Bethsaida Temple and every other week I traveled to and from Chicago, where I was the pastor of The Original Church of God located at 72nd and

♦ ♦ ♦

Preface
The Office of the Prophet

Racine on the South Side of Chicago for 2½ years. One day while waiting for a flight, the Lord spoke again, "Leslie, I have people right here in this city that I want you to reach for me. You do not have to travel over 900 miles, one-way, to preach."

After a serious conversation with Dr. Holiman, I planted the ministry of My Father's House International Christian Discipleship Center in Aurora, Colorado (we are now located in Denver, Colorado). In March 1996, we held our first service. The Lord has been gracious to me by entrusting me with the responsibility to oversee His precious work.

It is my prayer that you will be able to glean something from the revelation contained in this book, "The Office of the Prophet." The Lord placed upon my heart "not to build a steeple, but to build people." He has therefore instilled within me the

Preface
The Office of the Prophet

ministry of discipleship. The tenor of this book and all that I do in ministry is to "equip people to do the will of God."

♦ ♦ ♦

THE OFFICE OF THE PROPHET

♦ ♦ ♦

CHAPTER 1

THE TESTIMONY OF JESUS CHRIST

Revelation 19:10 says in part, *"... for the testimony of Jesus is the spirit of prophecy."* What does it mean to have the testimony of Jesus Christ? I believe John is saying that we must not only know *of* Jesus Christ, but we must be known *by* Him or we must be in covenant with Jesus Christ. In other words, we must have more than just a "head knowledge" or an intellectual knowledge of Jesus Christ, but we must also have a covenant bond with Him just as a man is "to have and to hold" his bride. The servants of Christ must go beyond the veil and enter the Holy of Holies. There must be an exchange of spirit for spirit—covenant is to go beyond the veil.

♦ ♦ ♦

Chapter 1— The Testimony of Jesus Christ
The Office of the Prophet

Note the messenger's powerful imagery in **Revelation 19:9: *"... Blessed [are] they which are called unto the marriage supper of the Lamb."*** The key word is "marriage," or "to have and to hold." When we are born again, it is our spirit that is born again. The soul and body are not completely changed until the total process of regeneration takes place. Therefore, the soul learns to think from the position of a "new creature." Once this takes place, the body begins to line up and transform.

A person who has the testimony of Jesus Christ most likely will also have a prophetic unction, but does not yet know how to express it or does not have a platform on which to release it. As it relates to the expression "to have and to hold," when a person has become impregnated with the testimony of Jesus Christ, they will begin to make necessary adjustments in their lives—as one who is pregnant begins to make

Chapter 1— The Testimony of Jesus Christ
The Office of the Prophet

changes. This is exactly what has taken place; the mindset is changed, which is a clear indicator that they have come into contact with the Risen Savior. Therefore, they are fertilized with something that will be manifested in time.

When a person is impregnated with the testimony of Jesus Christ, everyone and everything around him is affected. That explains why John, after seeing the angel, wanted to fall down and worship him (we must be careful not to misuse this awesome presence). Notice that John wanted to fall down, but the angel or messenger instructed John to worship God. Even though the Apostle John was in the Spirit,[7] he still needed to hear a prophetic voice to obtain direction about what he do.

---

[7] Revelation 1:10

Chapter 1— The Testimony of Jesus Christ
The Office of the Prophet

The messenger told John that ***"I am thy fellowservant, and of thy brethren that have the testimony of Jesus …."*** This is significant because John was the apostle and messenger to the church at this particular time in history. When both the apostolic and prophetic come forth they work hand-in-hand. They work in synchronic unity and not separately. Once the prophetic voice was released and order was achieved, the heavens opened and John saw the vision.[8] What a powerful passage of scripture!

In a covenant relationship, there must first be an exchange of vows or a covenant spoken. Following this exchange is a consummation (or completion) of the vows—an exchange of spirit to spirit; I refer to this as "kingdom commerce." This puts one in a position to have the testimony of Jesus Christ. This connecting of both the

---

[8] Revelation 1:11

Chapter 1— The Testimony of Jesus Christ
The Office of the Prophet

apostolic and prophetic was illustrated by the messenger when he declared to John that he was his brother and fellow servant. Here, we see clearly the connectedness of the apostolic and the prophetic. After the two come together, they produce life!

The Bible says ***For with the heart man believeth unto righteousness; and with the mouth confession is made unto salvation.*** (**Romans 10:10**) When a man believes and confesses faith, he is then able to enter beyond the veil. The scripture says in **1 John 5:7-10**:

> ***For there are three that bear record in heaven, the Father, the Word, and the Holy Ghost: and these three are one. And there are three that bear witness in earth, the Spirit, and the water, and the blood: and these three agree in one. If we receive***

♦ ♦ ♦

Chapter 1— The Testimony of Jesus Christ
The Office of the Prophet

> ***the witness of men, the witness of God is greater: for this is the witness of God which he hath testified of his Son. He that believeth on the Son of God hath the witness in himself: he that believeth not God hath made him a liar; because he believeth not the record that God gave of his Son.***

In Christendom we often observe individuals attempting to operate in different offices—at the same time. My belief is that this is primarily due to the lack of understanding and insecurity. Many pastors are apostles, but they are fearful of the prophetic. Therefore, when the Spirit moves in the midst of their congregations, they "catch the wave" without fully understanding what is taking place. When this happens, it is because those leaders have

♦ ♦ ♦

Chapter 1— The Testimony of Jesus Christ
The Office of the Prophet

become intimidated by their lack of understanding of the prophetic rhythms. In this environment leaders will often employ "church as usual" tactics such as to sing traditional hymns or other songs in an effort to harness the spirit.

Today there are many who declare they are called to the office of the prophet and who feel the urge in their spirit that God indeed is speaking His divine oracles to them and through them.[9] Later in the text, I will address the negative connotation in which many are unaware that they are operating in the area of familiar spirits. The Apostle Paul warns that there would be a great falling away (renunciation of Christ) with many descending into a state of apostasy.[10]

---

[9] The prophetic gifting is not gender specific. *(See* Acts 21:9.) I write in masculine form for the sake of ease.

[10] 2 Thessalonians 2:2-3

Chapter 1— The Testimony of Jesus Christ
The Office of the Prophet

This book is mandatory for the prophet of God who holds sacred and dear the office of his calling and who understands Jude's warning: ***For there are certain men crept in unawares, who were before of old ordained to this condemnation, ungodly men, turning the grace of our God into lasciviousness, and denying the only Lord God, and our Lord Jesus Christ.*** **(Jude 4)**

I believe it is very important for every leader in the Body of Christ to embrace the operation and role of this essential office. Familiarizing ourselves with the truth of God's word gives us a fighting chance to be able to discern the difference between the true prophets of God and false prophets.

When one has indeed been called to the office of the prophet, they recognize that they stand in the presence of God. In **2 Kings 3:14**, as Elisha addressed both King

Chapter 1— The Testimony of Jesus Christ
The Office of the Prophet

Jehoshaphat and King Jehoram (King of Israel), he proclaimed that he was standing before the Lord. The phrase "to stand before the Lord" in scripture indicates one who is positioned and qualified to judge in the earth.

For example, shortly before Stephen's death, he looked up into heaven and saw the Lord standing on the right hand of God judging his persecutors.[11] Another illustration is the example of the woman taken in adultery and brought before Jesus by the zealous scribes and Pharisees. Because Jesus was standing in accordance with the authority of the prophetic rhythms of heaven, He challenged their own blamelessness. One by one, each of the woman's accusers walked away, tormented

---

[11] Acts 7:55

Chapter 1— The Testimony of Jesus Christ
The Office of the Prophet

and ashamed because of their own guilt-ridden consciences.[12]

When the anointing is flowing, *anyone* can be used by the Spirit of Prophecy. However, one must be born of water and of the Spirit.[13] No one can have the testimony of Jesus Christ without going beyond the veil. Of course, going beyond the veil requires one to reveal himself and to become transparent. Until we reveal ourselves before The Lamb, He will not reveal Himself to us. As God's creation, we must be open and naked before Him. It is only then that we can truly call Him our High Priest.[14] When He beckons, then and only then, can we go beyond the veil.

---

[12] St. John 8:1-11

[13] St. John 3;5

[14] Hebrews 4:13-14

♦ ♦ ♦

Chapter 1— The Testimony of Jesus Christ
The Office of the Prophet

Questions *(Provide scripture references where applicable)*:

1. What is the Testimony of Jesus Christ?

2. How has the Testimony of Jesus Christ been revealed in your life and in your ministry?

3. Why is it necessary for the prophet of God to have his own personal testimony of Jesus Christ?

4. What is the importance of harmony and unity among the prophetic and the apostolic?

5. Have you ever had an encounter with the prophetic rhythms of heaven?

6. Why is there often a fear of the prophetic?

♦ ♦ ♦

Chapter 1— The Testimony of Jesus Christ
The Office of the Prophet

7. How does the prophet of God differentiate the true prophetic from the operation of familiar spirits?

Chapter 1— The Testimony of Jesus Christ
The Office of the Prophet

♦   ♦   ♦

THE OFFICE OF THE PROPHET

♦　　♦　　♦

CHAPTER 2

THE ORIGIN OF THE OFFICE OF THE PROPHET

Historically, we have understood the prophet from the context of dispensations, and not as a sovereign operation of the plan of God.[15] The Bible clearly says in **Amos 3:7,** *"Surely the Lord GOD will do nothing, but he revealeth his secret unto his servants the prophets."*

The word servant is interesting. The Hebrew word for servant is *ebed*[16] and the

---

[15] King James Bible, *Bible Survey: Prophets, Poetry, and Wisdom*: Thomas Nelson Inc. (1988)

[16] Jewish Encyclopedia (1906), *Slaves and Slavery.* Retrieved from http://www.jewishencyclopedia.com/articles/13799-slaves-and-slavery.

♦　　♦　　♦

Chapter 2—The Origin of the Office of the Prophet
The Office of the Prophet

Greek word is *doulos*.[17] In both languages, the basic use of the word means "one who gives himself up to another's will." Amos, one of the Twelve Minor Prophets, was a sheep herder and a farmer of the sycamore fig. But the Lord God called Amos from his natural occupations into the prophetic rhythms of heaven. Amos responded to the call of God, but it required a complete surrender of his life and of everything that he knew. He was given a compulsory assignment: warn Israel of their sins! It is very important to note here that as the Lord called and commissioned the men of God, He sent the men of God. From this we must understand that the apostolic and the prophetic are synonymous counterparts of each other.

---

[17] New Testament Greek Lexicon (King James Version). Retrieved from
http://www.biblestudytools.com/lexicons/greek/nas/doulos.html.

♦ ♦ ♦

Chapter 2—The Origin of the Office of the Prophet
The Office of the Prophet

Amos had three colossal tasks that enjoined both the apostolic and the prophetic: (1) study and scrutinize the immorality of Israel and the surrounding nations, (2) explicitly identify the transgressions of the Israelites, and (3) unequivocally warn the Israelites that they would not escape God's judgment for their idolatrous and immoral lifestyles.

The prophetic voice or Word of God makes things happen both on earth and in the heavens. Without a word spoken nothing takes place. As thought is communicated in the spirit realm, those thoughts are translated into words. Finally, the sounds of thought are crystallized in the spirit—the prophetic rhythms of God. In the beginning God spoke and things happened! After His spoken word, He declared that ***"there is not a man to till the ground,"***[18] or to do my bidding on

---

[18] Genesis 2:5

Chapter 2—The Origin of the Office of the Prophet
The Office of the Prophet

the earth. Therefore, He said, "Let us make man in our image, after our likeness ...."[19] Elohim revealed this pattern as He created the heavens and the earth. In this moment the prophetic rhythms of God were crystallized *"ex nihilo"*[20] or out of nothing. His desires came into existence forthright! When the prophet of God recognizes that he stands in the very presence of God, he recognizes that he needs nothing else to fulfill the will of God. He simply speaks into the atmosphere what is revealed from heaven and heaven sanctions the will of God in the earth.

It is God's will that matters. God says in **Isaiah 55:8**:

---

[19] Genesis 1:26-27

[20] Origin of *ex nihilo:* Latin for "from or out of nothing." *Webster's Third New International Dictionary of the English Language*, unabridged. Merriam-Webster, Inc. (1993).

◆ ◆ ◆

Chapter 2—The Origin of the Office of the Prophet
The Office of the Prophet

> ***For my thoughts are not your thoughts, neither are your ways my ways, saith the LORD. For as the heavens are higher than the earth, so are my ways higher than your ways, and my thoughts than your thoughts.***

In this passage of Scripture the writer is neither addressing the children of God nor His servants—the writer addresses the wicked. Many refer to this passage of Scripture, but it has been misinterpreted by infiltrators who want to encourage us to believe that it is referring to the thoughts of Christians, or of God's children. Many other Scriptures reveal that one purpose for Christ's coming is to reveal the will of God in the earth. **Philippians 2:5** exhorts the believer to "*Let this mind be in you, which was also in Christ Jesus*." Paul presents and answers the question in **1 Corinthians 2:16**:

♦ ♦ ♦

Chapter 2—The Origin of the Office of the Prophet
The Office of the Prophet

"*For who hath known the mind of the Lord, that he may instruct him? But we have the mind of Christ.*"

Jesus Christ came so that we could have the mind of God and so that we can speak His will in the earth. Just as it was necessary for Christ to be crucified at Calvary, we too must crucify our thoughts. Once we crucify our own thoughts, we are ready to receive the revelation of the mind of God so that we can speak His will in the earth.

God assigned Adam many tasks, among which was to speak into existence the names of the every living creature.[21] Whatever name Adam spoke that would be the name thereof. The prophetic word has always identified what God did from the beginning. The prophetic voice was always

---

[21] Genesis 2:19

Chapter 2—The Origin of the Office of the Prophet
The Office of the Prophet

intended to identify the workings or the will of God in the earth, as well as in the heavens. All things began with a sound and all things will culminate with a sound—the prophetic voice.[22] Let's take a look at some examples.

First, remember when God came seeking Adam? The Bible says that Adam heard the voice of the Lord walking in the cool of the day.[23] This is an anthropomorphic term describing the characteristics of God in terms of human behavior. Let's consider this: The Lord asked Adam, ***"Where art thou?"***[24] Note that Adam does not respond right away. He hides himself from the voice of God or, in other words, from the prophetic voice of God. When the voice of God is moving in the

---

[22] 1 Thessalonians 4:16

[23] Genesis 3:8

[24] Genesis 3:9

Chapter 2—The Origin of the Office of the Prophet
The Office of the Prophet

earth, sin is always revealed. Adam was the prophetic voice in the earth to identify all things. But because of sin, there was an interruption in the voice of the prophetic. God came to deal with that sin in a strong way.

This is why it is especially important that the prophet of God know how to protect his God-given gift. (*See* Chapter 7, How to Protect This Gift) Disobedience in the prophet of God will cause an interruption of the pure flow of the prophetic rhythms of heaven in the prophet's life. This is consistent throughout Scripture—when the prophet of God failed to obey God, God sent His words by a prophet to correct the disobedient prophet.

David is highly regarded as one of the prophets sent by God to govern the Israelites—David was king and prophet as well as a prolific poet and musician. Although David was a man after God's own

Chapter 2—The Origin of the Office of the Prophet
The Office of the Prophet

heart, his life was a dichotomy: he was steadfast and tenacious in his commitment to God, but at the same time guilty of some of the most serious sins recorded in the Old Testament. David's clashing proclivities disrupted the prophetic rhythms of God in his life. David sinned against God with Bathsheba,[25] the daughter of Eliam, and ordered her husband Uriah killed in battle.[26] In His great displeasure, God sent another prophet, Nathan, with a word of correction and reproof.[27] The same prophet who delivered a word of blessing to David in **2 Samuel 7**, now used his prophetic voice to bring conviction to David's heart.

Next we see Noah, another prophet of God, who was in alignment with Amos 3:7. He was the prophetic voice in the earth

---

[25] 2 Samuel 11:4

[26] 2 Samuel 11:15

[27] 2 Samuel 12.1-12

Chapter 2—The Origin of the Office of the Prophet
The Office of the Prophet

with a message from God. The Lord revealed to Noah what His plans were for the earth. Let us not lose sight of the fact that God uses the prophetic voice in the earth to declare His will on the earth, as it is in heaven.

This prophet preached for years as he prepared an Ark according to the Lord's instructions. Noah's congregation consisted of his family (eight souls,[28] including himself).[29] Outside of his family, Noah had no other converts. Noah was not only a preacher and a prophet, but he was also a priest who offered sacrifices unto God.[30] God used Noah in multiple capacities. It is my belief that God, in His sovereignty, will use the prophet in more than one capacity. This is exciting because it is at this moment

---

[28] 1 Peter 3:20

[29] 2 Peter 2:5

[30] Genesis 8:20

♦ ♦ ♦

Chapter 2—The Origin of the Office of the Prophet
The Office of the Prophet

that we begin to see a glimpse or a foreshadowing of the fivefold ministry!

Next let's consider Abram, the friend of God.[31] This prophet, chosen by God, had a powerful prophetic voice in the earth. Although chosen, Abram still had to learn a few things. Even so, the Lord proclaimed that He would bless him who blessed Abram, and curse him who cursed Abram.[32] There were multiple dimensions and multiple layers related to Abram's calling. Not only was he a prophet of God, but he was also a priest and an apostle. More importantly, he was a servant of the Most High God. God gave Abram a word to carry forth and upon receiving this word, Abram became the prophet of God. God revealed to him what His plan was for the earth and after several mistakes, Abram got it right!

---

[31] Isaiah 41:8

[32] Genesis 12:3

Chapter 2—The Origin of the Office of the Prophet
The Office of the Prophet

One mistake Abram made was that he lied to King Abimelech and deceitfully proclaimed that Sarah was his sister.[33] In a dream, the Lord revealed to the king that Abram had deceived him and revealed that Abram was a prophet.[34] God then instructed Abimelech to do right by Abram and to restore his wife to him. Although it was Abram who deceived the king, God instructed the king to have Abram pray for his wife and for the kingdom. After the prophet prayed for King Abimelech, God opened the womb of his wife. When Abimelech returned Sarah to Abram in obedience to the voice of the prophet, God blessed his kingdom.[35]

Perhaps you have never considered Abraham as a prophet of God, but the Scripture clearly calls him a prophet of God.

---

[33] Genesis 20:2

[34] Genesis 20:3-7

[35] Genesis 20:17

♦ ♦ ♦

Chapter 2—The Origin of the Office of the Prophet
The Office of the Prophet

In **Genesis 20:7**, the Lord spoke to Abimelech, "*Now therefore restore the man his wife; for he is a prophet, and he shall pray for thee, and thou shalt live: and if thou restore her not, know thou that thou shalt surely die, thou, and all that are thine.*" Abraham was sent by God, with a word from God. This illustration provides us great insight into the apostolic and prophetic synchronization.

The Old Testament books of Isaiah through Daniel are identified as the "major prophets." However, the prophetic office operated long before these were defined. As a matter of fact, all prophetic offices are considered "major" because God uses them to reveal His plans. As you continue reading, it will become clear that the office of the prophet did not just appear on the scene when Isaiah appeared on the scene.

It is important to "think outside the box" as it relates to this particular subject,

♦ ♦ ♦

Chapter 2—The Origin of the Office of the Prophet
The Office of the Prophet

because God only has one will—that His plan in the earth be completed. He uses ways that are not our ways to carry out His plan in the earth.

Questions *(Provide scripture references where applicable)*:

1. Where can the origin of the office of the prophet be traced?

2. How are the foundational principles of that dispensation relevant today?

3. What is your testimony concerning the origin or beginning of prophecy in your personal experience with God?

4. Describe how the various dimensions and layers of prophecy have impacted our world history?

♦ ♦ ♦

Chapter 2—The Origin of the Office of the Prophet
The Office of the Prophet

5. What three prophets of God from the Tribe of Levi are mentioned in the Torah (the first five books of the Old Testament)?

6. Which Old Testament prophet prayed that Abimelech's wife would conceive and bear children?

♦ ♦ ♦

Chapter 2—The Origin of the Office of the Prophet
The Office of the Prophet

_____

_____

_____

_____

_____

_____

_____

♦   ♦   ♦

THE OFFICE OF THE PROPHET

♦ ♦ ♦

CHAPTER 3

THE AUDIENCE OF THE PROPHET

This chapter is very important to the office of the prophet. Who is the prophet sent to speak and who is his audience? It is vital that the prophet fully understand his mission. Young prophets often do not immediately understand to whom they are to prophesy. I believe this is one reason why Jesus stated to His disciples that He was sent to the lost sheep of the Israel.[36] Jesus knew who His audience was—without any doubt. However, He had to identify for His disciples their audience.[37]

---

[36] St. Matthew 15:24

[37] St. Matthew 10:6

Chapter 3—The Audience of the Prophet
The Office of the Prophet

I believe this is one reason the Old Testament model of the school of the prophets was pivotal. Having in place the apostolic headship of a seasoned prophet can assist in helping to identify the audience of the prophet. (*See* Chapter 4 for further discussion about the school of the prophets)

In the Old Testament God clearly identified for His prophets their audience. They did not have to guess to whom they were sent to preach. This is a critical aspect of the prophetic office that many prophets often miss. As a practical matter, perhaps the Lord will challenge you in this area to reconsider to whom you should be preaching.

Consider Noah who preached to a wicked generation.[38] Even though Noah had a message directly from God, the people

---

[38] St. Matthew 24:37-38

Chapter 3—The Audience of the Prophet
The Office of the Prophet

would not listen to him. We see this pattern often repeated. Abram had to leave his father's house and go to a land where he did not know the people.[39] Lot's audience was in Sodom and Gomorrah.[40] Moses went to Pharaoh in Egypt.[41] Each had to preach in a desert place to a people who would not listen. God warned Jeremiah in advance that although the people would not listen to him, his task was to declare the Word of God, regardless of the expression on their faces.[42] Ezekiel was told to set his face like a flint and to not be dismayed.[43] Instead, he was to say "what thus sayeth the Lord."

Young prophets often want to address a kind and gentle audience, without

---

[39] Genesis 12:1

[40] Genesis 13:10-11

[41] Exodus 4:21

[42] Jeremiah 1:17

[43] Ezekiel 3:9

Chapter 3—The Audience of the Prophet
The Office of the Prophet

a good understanding of the weight of the message that the messenger intends to convey. The Prophet Malachi was one of the last of the twelve Minor Prophets whose name means "messenger of the Most High," or "God's messenger." Malachi is an example of one who understood his purpose, who respected the One who sent him, and who knew who his audience was.

In Malachi 1:1, Malachi introduced himself with this statement, ***"The burden of the word of the LORD to Israel by Malachi."*** Malachi's audience was tough— probably one of the toughest audiences that a prophet could have! Many Christians focus more on Malachi's reference to tithes than to any of the other issues that he addresses concerning their overall negligence and regarding their religious, family and social duties.[44] Malachi identifies his audience in

---

[44] Malachi 3:8-10

Chapter 3—The Audience of the Prophet
The Office of the Prophet

Malachi 2:1: *"And now, O ye priests, this commandment is for you."* Malachi's message was directed to the leaders in Israel who had failed in their responsibility to teach the people how to reverence God in their sacrificial giving. Now we understand why his audience was so tough; he was addressing leaders. Throughout the remainder of the book, Malachi reproves his audience—all of the Israelites—but in particular, the priests of Israel.

Elijah the Tishbite is another example. The Prophet Elijah came from Gilead to Israel to deliver his first message to a king—a king who had the power to kill him! But Elijah boldly declared to King Ahab that, *"… As the LORD God of Israel liveth, before whom I stand, there shall not be dew nor rain these years, but according to my word."* (**1 Kings 17:1**)

On another occasion, Elijah met Obadiah who was a governor of the House

♦ ♦ ♦

Chapter 3—The Audience of the Prophet
The Office of the Prophet

of Ahab and who feared the Lord.[45] Obadiah had the gift of prophecy and Elijah charged him to go before him and announce his arrival.[46] Obadiah was so shaken by this task of taking this message to the king, that he thought he had sinned and that King Ahab would surely kill him.[47] This particular exchange illustrates that when a prophet is sent by God to people of power and influence, they can impact time and bring about change to the circumstances of the poor and the underclass. For example, Moses spoke to Pharaoh about the bondage of the children of Israel. Nehemiah's sadness concerning the Jewish people and Jerusalem's vulnerability because of a lack of defense touched the heart of King Artaxerxes. The Prophet Nathan confronted David for stealing from the defenseless. And

---

[45] 1 Kings 18:3

[46] 1 Kings 18:8

[47] 1 Kings 18:9

Chapter 3—The Audience of the Prophet
The Office of the Prophet

Isaiah counseled that if Hezekiah made no ungodly alliances but trusted only in the Lord, it would be well for his nation and for his people.

Almost without exception, the Old Testament prophets of God were sent to those in authority and those who had the power to decree laws as well as to influence regional climates. It was imperative for the prophet to seek God before prophesying to the king. Young prophets can be so anxious to exercise their gift that they speak before receiving proper training and mentorship by seasoned prophets. Subsequently, they are reckless and end up casting their pearls before swine.[48] In other words, the gift of prophesy is a pearl from God; it is valuable and must be handled with care and superior stewardship. Prophesying at the wrong time or to the wrong audience will cause the word

---

[48] Matthew 7;6

Chapter 3—The Audience of the Prophet
The Office of the Prophet

of God to be despised and rejected. Likewise, the prophet must be prepared to handle the rejection that is often the result of declaring God's word.

Thus, the prophet of God must keenly be able to identify his audience with the skill and accuracy of a sharpshooter. If you believe that you are called to the office of the prophet and that God has revealed to you an apostolic and prophetic word, you first must ask: Who is my audience? Second, you must ask: Where is the region of influence of my audience? These questions will be effective in helping you to locate your audience. Always remember that God will identify your audience as He sends you.

The office of the prophet is forever relevant and imperative to all people. However, although the prophetic purpose is yet in motion, it can be perverted. A wise person in authority, or one who starts a new venture, will seek direction before

♦ ♦ ♦

proceeding with what is in their heart. The President of the United States has advisors, chief executive officers have advisors, and chief financial officers have advisors. *"For by wise counsel thou shalt make thy war: and in multitude of counsellors there is safety."* **(Proverbs 24:6)**

The structure of the prophetic office is from heaven, and God wants the Church of the living God to be the Church! The Church has been given a voice in the earth. Unfortunately, many cannot discern that voice. It is important that we hear and discern that voice. **1 Corinthians 14:7** describes the importance of discerning that voice: *"And even things without life giving sound, whether pipe or harp, except they give a distinction in the sounds, how shall it be known what is piped or harped?"* If the voice is not distinct, people will not know whether to prepare for war or for celebration, or whether to mourn or to weep.

♦ ♦ ♦

Chapter 3—The Audience of the Prophet
The Office of the Prophet

When the devil wants to confuse a people, he comes along side of what God is saying and tries to distort the sound. He recognizes that if he can distort the sound, he can persuade the prophet to consider what he is saying. He then can persuade the prophet to say what he wants him to say, and not what God wants him to say.

Since the prophet has been given authority in the earth, God needs him to say what He wants done. There is a powerful lesson in this. Only God can call those things which be not as though they were.[49] However, God has granted us a power of attorney ("POA") in the earth to speak on His behalf. Therefore, as God's agents, we have the ability and the power to emphatically declare what God has said, and it is so!

---

[49] Romans 4:17

♦ ♦ ♦

Chapter 3—The Audience of the Prophet
The Office of the Prophet

It is beautiful to note that when we speak the prophetic rhythms of heaven, all of heaven is ready and anxious to respond. The defeated one does not have this ability. This is one reason why [s]atan[50] visited man in the Garden of Eden; he recognized man's authority. [s]atan needs man to speak for him.

These principles operate both in the spirit world and in the natural. In the natural, we call them laws. When a law is written, a king or one in authority must decree it. Once a king issues an official order of decree, it becomes law—an enforceable rule. This natural concept works the same way in the spirit. [s]atan needs our official endorsement because he recognizes that we are the kings and priests on the earth.[51] He respects the authority represented by the POA granted to

---

[50] Although the name [s]atan is a proper noun, I choose to make reference to him as [s]atan in my book.

[51] Psalms 115:16; 1 Peter 2:9; Revelation 5:10; Revelation 21:24

♦ ♦ ♦

Chapter 3—The Audience of the Prophet
The Office of the Prophet

us by God. He respects that power in the earth realm and he understands that nothing can be accomplished in the earth without a word spoken first. [s]atan tries every tactic he knows to try to convince us to speak on his behalf. One tactic is that he sends his spirits to entice both the saved and the unsaved to speak his thoughts. While prophetically we understand this principle, sadly we fail to teach this message in our churches. Why? We have become so concerned about the things of this world that we have failed to acknowledge that we must fulfill our divine assignment in the earth. ***In whom the god of this world hath blinded the minds of them which believe not, lest the light of the glorious gospel of Christ, who is the image of God, should shine unto them. (2 Corinthians 4:4)***

As God's agents who have the authority to speak into the earth, it is imperative that we (1) are sure who our

♦ ♦ ♦

audience is, (2) are careful and circumspect, and (3) use great discernment with what we allow to flow from our mouths. Once a word is spoken from the mouth of the prophet, whether good or evil, it is released into the atmosphere.

My Prophetic Pathway

In 1992 while employed by the airlines, I received notice that I would be transferred to Omaha, Nebraska. So I moved my family from Denver and we headed to Omaha. I was excited about this new adventure thinking in my mind that perhaps God wanted me to plant a church. It was also during this time that the Lord inspired the name of a new radio broadcast, "Crying in the Wilderness" (the name of all of my subsequent broadcasting programs). So I began the process of seeking an audience. I did not realize that it would not be easy and that I would first experience many things before I could accurately discern my audience.

As I ministered both on radio and television in Omaha, people began to tune in regularly and the program received a fair amount of positive feedback.

♦ ♦ ♦

Chapter 3—The Audience of the Prophet
The Office of the Prophet

> Shortly after the commencement of "Crying in the Wilderness," the Lord opened the door for me to pastor my first congregation in Chicago, Illinois. There I began to pastor the members of The Original Church of God located at 72nd Avenue. This proved to be an incredible experience and I am eternally grateful that the Lord ordered my steps to the south side of Chicago to lead this awesome ministry. Although small, the Lord had sent me to my first audience and it was here that I began to understand the synchronicity of the apostolic and prophetic call of God.
>
> I commuted back and forth between Omaha and Chicago to provide leadership to this congregation for over two and half years. By this time, my family and I had returned to Denver. One day while at the airport on my way to Chicago, the Lord spoke to me, "Leslie, I have people right here in this city and I want you to reach them for me. You do not have to travel over 900 miles each way to preach. There are people right here in Denver that you must reach."
>
> After a time of prayer and fasting, I had a serious conversation with my apostolic covering, Bishop Holiman. I explained to him God's message and he encouraged me to obey the voice of God. As I

Chapter 3—The Audience of the Prophet
The Office of the Prophet

> walked in obedience, God began to reveal who would be my audience in Denver.
>
> I admit that when My Father's House International Christian Discipleship Center was planted, I did not know what I know today about the prophetic. At the conception of My Father's House, I still did not know my audience (I had not yet met 99% of the members who attend this ministry today). But after 17 years and still going strong, the Lord has helped me to understand my audience and to recognize the gifts in the members of my church. Over time and after living the principles written in this book, God has anointed me to prophesy to His people instantly and with precision.

Questions *(Provide scripture references where applicable)*:

1. What is the structure of the office of the prophet?

2. How has God confirmed in your life when you were to speak

♦ ♦ ♦

Chapter 3—The Audience of the Prophet
The Office of the Prophet

> prophetically to a particular individual or group?

3. How does the prophet distinguish the voice of God from the voice of [s]atan?

4. Why is it vitally important that the prophet of God know how to discern who is his audience?

5. What important questions must the prophet ask himself before going forth to speak a word from the Lord?

6. What prerequisites must be met by the prophet of God to position him to be able to speak forth the will of God?

♦ ♦ ♦

Chapter 3—The Audience of the Prophet
The Office of the Prophet

_____

_____

_____

_____

_____

_____

_____

♦   ♦   ♦

THE OFFICE OF THE PROPHET
♦ ♦ ♦

CHAPTER 4

<u>LOCATING THE PROPHETIC VOICE</u>

In this chapter, I discuss the significance of the location of the prophetic voice. If the prophet is confused about location, the prophet will be operating out of order and at the wrong position. This is not an easy concept to grasp, but I will do my best to explain it.

Throughout scripture we see that it is God's desire that His voice be represented in the earth. Whenever there was a need for something to be done, God raised up an apostolic/prophetic voice. This voice spoke His will with the purpose of impacting masses of people, primarily people who were oppressed and in trouble. Therefore, the essential purpose of the prophetic voice

Chapter 4—Locating the Prophetic Voice
The Office of the Prophet

is to release those who are oppressed. From Moses'[52] time to the arrival of Jesus,[53] and even today, that purpose has not changed.

This leads us to ask a reasonable question: Where is the prophetic voice located? Surprisingly, that voice often is not located where you think it would be—it is located at the seat of influence. As we travel back in time to the Old Testament, we see that every king had to deal with the prophetic voice—godly kings and pagan kings. While it will not be comfortable, the prophet must be prepared for threats and rejection. It is, therefore, necessary for the prophet to be positioned where he can have the greatest impact.

I believe that we have really gotten off track. Many who are called and have

---

[52] Exodus 3:11-15

[53] St. Luke 4:18

♦   ♦   ♦

Chapter 4—Locating the Prophetic Voice
The Office of the Prophet

been given the prophetic voice in the earth understand this office from a limited dimension—that they are called only to prophesy in the church. This sounds good and it is certainly one dimension of the office of the prophet. However, prophesying in the church is definitely not the only dimension that God intends. The Church has become limited in its vision; we have failed to recognize that there are other prophetic dimensions. There are many prophetic voices speaking in the earth. These voices are impacting the world in a very positive way for the Kingdom of God.

The reason you are reading this book now is because a prophetic voice was released in the earth. That voice spoke a word and sent it to the publishing company. A prophetic voice spoke a word concerning the distribution and marketing of this book. The laws that have been decreed on behalf

Chapter 4—Locating the Prophetic Voice
The Office of the Prophet

of freedom of speech allow this voice to be spread throughout the earth.

When a prophetic voice is released in the earth, it is a blessing to every nation. Unfortunately, not every prophetic voice is released for the right reason. Prophets are to speak from a seat of influence, not out of the shadows of obscurity. When the prophetic voice is locked away in a house, God's intended impact in the earth is not accomplished.

God sent Elijah to King Ahab with a prophetic warning that it would not rain for three years. That same prophetic voice released a directive to the Prophet Obadiah to come out of his comfort zone—come out of hiding and go tell King Ahab that Elijah is in town!

Although Obadiah was brave enough to hide 100 prophets of the Lord in a cave

♦ ♦ ♦

Chapter 4—Locating the Prophetic Voice
The Office of the Prophet

and to feed them from King Ahab's table,[54] he was afraid to speak to Ahab. He was doing a good thing by protecting the prophets of the Lord, but God required more of him. God was concerned about the seven thousand knees who had not bowed unto or kissed Baal—they needed to hear a prophetic voice![55] I believe God's specific purpose in sending Elijah to King Ahab was so that the prophetic voices that were hidden in the cave would be released.

There are many prophets with the Obadiah spirit—he was employed by the house of Ahab, yet he took bread from Jezebel's table to feed the prophets of the Lord.

In this passage of Scripture we witness the prophetic voice fearfully hiding

---

[54] 1 Kings 18:4

[55] 1 Kings 19:18

Chapter 4—Locating the Prophetic Voice
The Office of the Prophet

away in seclusion. Concealing and withholding the prophetic voice must never become a prescribed standard for the prophet of God. The prophet must understand that the archenemy of the prophetic voice of God is—and always has been—the spirit of Jezebel.[56] The spirit of Jezebel recognizes that her demise has always been in the mouth of the Lord's prophets. The spirit of Jezebel rules when she can shut the mouths of the prophets of the Most High God while at the same time, secretly allow them to eat from her table—thereby prohibiting the voice of God from being released in the earth.

Inherent in the heart of the prophet should be a deep subconscious yearning to develop and cultivate the gift, as well as an innate desire to manage the gift with the spirit of excellence. But the prophet must

---

[56] Revelation 2:20

Chapter 4—Locating the Prophetic Voice
The Office of the Prophet

first be teachable. This teachable temperament should imitate that of the Ethiopian eunuch who traveled from the courts of Queen Candace to worship God at Jerusalem. God arranged a divine encounter between this man and the prophetic, Apostle Philip, so that Philip could teach and provide understanding. When Philip saw the man reading scripture, he asked if he was reading with an understanding. The Ethiopian humbly responded ***"How can I, except some man should guide me."*** **(Acts 8:31)** The Greek word *katécheó*[57] means "to catechize [and] teach[ing] foundational truths as they relate to progressing in the Christian life."[58] The Ethiopian lacked spiritual knowledge and comprehension and he lacked the spiritual capacity to understand who God is.

---

[57] Strong's Concordance (2727). Retrieved from http://biblesuite.com/greek/2727.htm.

[58] Galatians 6:6

♦ ♦ ♦

Chapter 4—Locating the Prophetic Voice
The Office of the Prophet

His humility and desire to learn about God led to his conversion.

Another example of learning to locate the prophetic voice can be seen in the life of Saul who required training and mentorship. **1 Samuel 9:27** portrays how God sent Saul to Samuel in the land of Zuph. Samuel shared with Saul all that God had given him, advised Saul that he was God's inaugural choice for creating a monarchy in Israel, and then privately anointed Saul as king.[59]

Although Saul was God's choice, Samuel let him know that he was not ready; he first needed additional training to prepare him to be both king and judge. Samuel told Saul that as he left his city, he would encounter three men on a journey to God to Bethel: one would carry three young goats,

---

[59] 1 Samuel 10:1

Chapter 4—Locating the Prophetic Voice
The Office of the Prophet

one would carry three loaves of bread, and one would carry a bottle of wine. He told Saul that these three men would greet him kindly and provide him sustenance needed for the next part of his journey. Saul would next find himself at the base of the military quarters of the Philistine army where he would meet a group of prophets praising God upon instruments and prophesying. Samuel next said that:

> *... [T]he Spirit of the LORD will come upon thee, and thou shalt prophesy with them, and shalt be turned into another man. And let it be, when these signs are come unto thee, that thou do as occasion serve thee; for God is with thee.* **(1 Samuel 10:6)**

Saul needed to experience the transformational effects of being in the

♦ ♦ ♦

Chapter 4—Locating the Prophetic Voice
The Office of the Prophet

presence of God. All who knew him recognized he was a changed man. That experience was a prolific teaching moment for Saul in the prophetic.

Although Saul received excellent training in the prophetic, his leadership was disappointing because he was bankrupt in the area of discipline; he was carnal more than he was spiritual; he was moody and unpredictable; he was persistently disobedient; and he lacked the character required to remain under the tutelage of the seasoned prophet Samuel. God therefore disqualified Saul, removed him from office as the governing leader of Israel, and commanded Samuel to train another man (David) to be God's new prophetic ambassador to speak the oracles of God. God loved His people and was not going to allow anyone to govern them who did not have a prophetic voice and a connection with heaven.

♦ ♦ ♦

Chapter 4—Locating the Prophetic Voice
The Office of the Prophet

Wherever great decisions are made that affect our daily lives, know that God has released a prophetic voice. Whenever God is moving in the earth, the devil is stirred up from below. For example, when the sons of God came before God's presence, [s]atan showed up too.[60] The discernment of the prophet of God must always be keen and acute as he moves in the prophetic thrust given by God in His Holiness. When the prophet speaks the divine oracles of God from above, he must anticipate that all that is beneath will become agitated, troubled, and disturbed.

You should also be aware that the devil releases a voice too! Because the gifts and callings of God are without repentance,[61] many times before a person comes to the saving knowledge of Jesus

---

[60] Job 2:1

[61] Romans 11:29

♦ ♦ ♦

Chapter 4—Locating the Prophetic Voice
The Office of the Prophet

Christ, they already have had tremendous influence over their environment and among their family and friends. However, once they are saved, they need someone to show them who they are and to teach them how to activate their prophetic gift. Training involves developing discernment, as well as cultivating and protecting the gift.

In the Old Testament, schools of the prophets were instituted so that the seasoned prophets could mentor and instruct the sons of the prophets. There were many schools such as the one in Gilgal, where the Prophet Elisha taught.[62]

We clearly see the connection between the location of the prophetic voice and the interactions between the prophets.

When one prophet comes into contact with another prophet, together they

---

[62] 2 Kings 4:38

♦ ♦ ♦

Chapter 4—Locating the Prophetic Voice
The Office of the Prophet

will stir up each other's gifts. This is what happens when one prophet speaks to another prophet:

> ***Let the prophets speak two or three, and let the other judge. If any thing be revealed to another that sitteth by, let the first hold his peace. For ye may all prophesy one by one, that all may learn, and all may be comforted. And the spirits of the prophets are subject to the prophets.*** **(1 Corinthians 14:29-32)**

The school of the prophets remains relevant throughout all ages. Prophets must acknowledge the importance of receiving instructions from seasoned prophets to properly develop and cultivate their gifts. In addition, they must not overlook the need for communion with each other.

♦ ♦ ♦

Chapter 4—Locating the Prophetic Voice
The Office of the Prophet

As we navigate our way from the Old Testament to the New Testament, the above-described pattern for locating the prophetic voice does not change. John the Baptist discovered that he was the voice of one crying in the wilderness.[63] At a trial before Agrippa and Festus, Paul bravely and enthusiastically defended the Gospel of Jesus Christ.[64] Paul faced an even more tough audience at Mars Hill where, with righteous indignation, he preached the truth to the Greek philosophers. Standing before the Chief Priests and the Sanhedrin, Pontius Pilate had a personal encounter with Jesus that forever changed his life. It was the prophetic voice which released Paul and Barnabas to their apostolic destinies.[65]

---

[63] St. Matthew 3:3

[64] Acts 26

[65] Acts 13:1-3

♦ ♦ ♦

Chapter 4—Locating the Prophetic Voice
The Office of the Prophet

I would like to make very clear when dealing with this subject of how to locate the prophetic voice, that it is incumbent upon the prophet to be prepared to stand in the presence of God. **2 Kings 3:14**. As the prophet Elisha referred to himself as one standing in the presence of God, when God calls the prophet, He judges the prophet's heart. God determines the prophet's readiness to be used in the earth as a voice *before* He reveals His prophetic secrets to the prophet.

In conclusion, it is imperative that the Prophet is willing to stand in the presence of God and have the secrets of his own heart judged by God before he is qualified to become the voice of God in the earth. Locating the prophetic voice is mandatory so that the prophet is able to exert influence to do the will of God by speaking to the powers of authority. Since

♦ ♦ ♦

Chapter 4—Locating the Prophetic Voice
The Office of the Prophet

the heart of the king is in the Lord's hand,[66] it is imperative that the king hear the prophetic voice of the prophet so that the righteousness of God will prevail.

> **My Prophetic Pathway**
>
> There are many instances in my life when God used me to speak His will—even before I knew Him or had learned how to locate His voice. On one occasion, my brother advised me of one of his friends who was having marital problems. He explained that his friend respected me and that it would be a good idea for me to reach out to him. With great reluctance, I decided to respond to my brother's request. On the way to this couple's home, I questioned my ability to counsel anyone with marital problems since I was separated from my wife. Nevertheless, upon arrival at this couple's home, my brother's friend warmly embraced me as if I were a long-lost friend. As I listened to the couple explain their problems, I received supernatural insight and divine instruction concerning their issues and I counseled them. They graciously received this counsel and I went my way.

---

[66] Proverbs 21:1

♦   ♦   ♦

Chapter 4—Locating the Prophetic Voice
The Office of the Prophet

> While discussing with them their marital issues, God began to convict my heart instructing me to go home to my wife and to practice at home what I had just "preached" to this couple.
>
> At that season in my life, I did not fully understand what I now know are the prophetic rhythms of heaven. My lack of spiritual understanding prohibited me from properly operating in the gifts that God had placed in me. After the Lord restored and filled me with the Holy Ghost in 1989, the logos of God appeared to me as I was reading Hebrews 4:1-2 with a call to ministry. He challenged me with these three questions: (1) What would you do if you saw a hole in the ground? (2) Would you allow people to fall into the hole? (3) People are dying and going to hell daily, what are you going do? To this day, I cannot articulate or fully describe the impact of that encounter with God. But from that moment on, the urgency and resolve to fully yield my life to the calling of God has never diminished and, in fact, it increases daily.
>
> Following this encounter during testimony services, I wanted to simply stand and share a brief sweet testimony like all of my brothers and sisters. But without fail when I stood among the congregation,

♦   ♦   ♦

Chapter 4—Locating the Prophetic Voice
The Office of the Prophet

> the spirit of God would fall upon me and I would prophesy. Retrospectively I understand what was happening, but at that time I had no idea that God was specifically calling me to the office of the prophet.
>
> An older, quieter and unassuming member in our congregation prophesied to me once during testimony service: "Brother Leslie, the Lord has called you and has placed His hand on you. You will be used of God mightily and many will not understand you because of the unusual and uncanny call on your life. Nevertheless, know that the Lord has called you and you must run for the Lord, my brother." I have lived to see every word she spoke come to pass.

Questions *(Provide scripture references where applicable)*:

1. Why, according to **1 Corinthians 14:29-32**, is order so necessary when the prophets of God are gathered together?

♦ ♦ ♦

Chapter 4—Locating the Prophetic Voice
The Office of the Prophet

2. Can you remember a time in your prophetic ministry when you were absolutely sure where your voice was needed at a particular time?

3. Can you identify situations where you could be called to prophesy beyond the walls of the church?

4. What safeguards must the prophet of God implement to guard against prophesying to the wrong audience?

5. What are the repercussions when the prophet of God speaks to the wrong audience?

♦ ♦ ♦

Chapter 4—Locating the Prophetic Voice
The Office of the Prophet

_____

_____

_____

_____

_____

_____

_____

♦   ♦   ♦

THE OFFICE OF THE PROPHET

♦ ♦ ♦

CHAPTER 5

HOW TO KNOW IF YOU ARE CALLED TO THE OFFICE OF THE PROPHET

Before you read this section, I want to caution you to not read it and suddenly proclaim that you are now a prophet. I encourage you first to seek God and then to confer with your apostolic covering. If you are sure that you have a prophetic calling and are no longer under the leadership of an apostolic authority, I encourage you to close this book, repent, and return to the last apostle you were under so that you can learn what you initially failed to learn. Prophets who refuse to submit to an apostle can be compared to a whore and God will bring judgment on them.

♦ ♦ ♦

Chapter 5—How to Know If You Are Called to the Office of the Prophet
The Office of the Prophet

To submit to and honor God's prophet is to submit to and honor Christ. There should be a high level of respect for leadership among the prophets of God. David understood this principle. Even though David may have been justified in bringing harm to King Saul for the injustices inflicted upon him by Saul, when the opportunity for revenge presented itself, David was convicted in his heart. The Bible says that **"his heart smote him because he had cut off Saul's skirt."**[67] Not only did David refuse to harm the king, but he would not allow anyone else to dishonor the first king of Israel—God's choice leader.[68]

Now, if you have not put down this book and are still reading, you are either curious or teachable—I pray it is the latter.

---

[67] 1 Samuel 24:5

[68] 1 Samuel 24:4-7

♦ ♦ ♦

Chapter 5—How to Know If You Are Called to the Office of the Prophet
The Office of the Prophet

The question most often asked by Christians is, "What is my calling?" Personally, I have to admit that it is frustrating to hear this question, because if God has called you, no one has to tell you—you will know. Many Christians who have been in the Church for years say they still do not know what their calling is. I want to help you with this: If you are saved, you are called. The calling of every Christian is to live a righteous life. You may say that you already know this, but if you fail to seek the kingdom of God, and His righteousness,[69] nothing will be added to you.

I believe that before the Lord can reveal to us our election, He must first deal with the foundational issue of salvation. We are often guilty of prematurely telling people that they have a ministry without first admonishing them that they must be born

---

[69] St. Matthew 6:33

Chapter 5—How to Know If You Are Called to the Office of the Prophet
The Office of the Prophet

again[70] and that they must live righteously. Without the full knowledge of what God requires of them, they will come to church seeking something from God without giving themselves wholly to Him.[71] If we are to be the mouthpiece for God, our lives must be exemplary and circumspect.

When a person shares with me that they have an unction that they are a prophet, I counsel them that they must first be proven. While I believe the fivefold ministry resides in each of us, we must remember that it is God who gives us the grace to operate in these offices. We do not have the luxury to choose in which office to operate. Our anointing is from God; He gets to make that decision![72]

---

[70] St. John 3:7

[71] 2 Corinthians 8:5

[72] 1 John 2:27

Chapter 5—How to Know If You Are Called to the Office of the Prophet
The Office of the Prophet

Contemporary prophets of God often get real excited when they read (and misinterpret) the phrase ***"a prophet's reward"*** in **Matthew 10:41**. Let me advise you that the reward of a prophet is not as attractive as one might believe. The biblical prophets of God were not surrounded by a large entourage of people like we see with some of today's mega "celebrity prophets." They were not showered with gifts, they did not live opulent lifestyles on lavish estates, nor did they have the material abundance that some believe are "rewards" of ministry. More often than not, they were persecuted by the "religious" and "irreligious" people of their day.

These prophets in fact could attest to how John must have felt after his banishment to the island of Patmos because of the testimony of Jesus Christ. They could commiserate with John—their companion in

♦   ♦   ♦

Chapter 5—How to Know If You Are Called to the Office of the Prophet
The Office of the Prophet

tribulations—[73]about their personal "Patmos" experiences. Patmos was not a vacation resort and cannot be compared to the luxury islands that we visit today such as the Islands of Italy, the Maldives, Turks and Caicos, St. Lucia, the island of Santorini and other Greek islands, to name a few. In contrast, the New Testament Greek Lexicon transliterates Patmos to mean "my killing"[74] because it was rugged, rocky, and jagged with especially harsh wildlife conditions. It was a bare island in the Aegean Sea that was desolate, volcanic, treeless, inhospitable, and forbidding. Therefore in my mind, a "Patmos experience" cannot in any way be equated to a reward. Although the Roman Empire penal system used Patmos as a place

---

[73] Revelation 1:9

[74] New Testament Greek Lexicon (King James Version). Retrieved from
(http://www.biblestudytools.com/search/?q=patmos&s=References&rc=LEX&rc2=LEX+GRK).

◆　　◆　　◆

of punishment to break the spirit of criminal and political prisoners who committed high treason, John was unlike any other prisoner because it was here at this banished place where he wrote the Gospel of St. John and the Book of Revelation.

So when a person says to me that they have a prophetic ministry, it is with solemnness of heart and with great compassion that I begin to intercede for them. Several years ago the Lord spoke to me that the age of the superstar Christian is over. The voice of God is released in the pews all over Christendom; sadly, His voice is becoming scarce in the pulpits.

The calling of a prophet (or seer) to deliver God's message for a specific purpose is unique and is different from one who exhorts or pastors. However, there often tends to be a natural progression for those called to the office of the prophet to believe

Chapter 5—How to Know If You Are Called to the Office of the Prophet
The Office of the Prophet

they must establish a church to operate in the calling of God. This is an extremely dangerous position and many precious years are wasted when those with a prophetic ministry attempt to operate as shepherds. The prophet must recognize that there is a difference in being called to protect and defend the sheep and in being called to proclaim the oracles of God.

In the days of old, the prophet was also called a seer. The Hebrew word for seer is *ra'ah*,[75] meaning to see, to perceive, to discern, and to have vision. It refers to one who sees into the supernatural and one who has immediate communication with God. ***"(Beforetime in Israel, when a man went to enquire of God, thus he spake, Come, and let us go to the seer: for he that is now***

---

[75] Old Testament Hebrew Lexicon (King James Version). Retrieved from http://www.biblestudytools.com/lexicons/hebrew/kjv/raah.html

Chapter 5—How to Know If You Are Called to the Office of the Prophet
The Office of the Prophet

called a Prophet was beforetime called a Seer.)" **(1 Samuel 9:9)**

Another Hebrew term *nābî* is correspondingly translated to mean "those through whom Adonai reveals His plans and messages.[76] Huehnergard writes that *nābî* is passively translated to mean "the one called."[77] Other transliterations of the word *nābî* mean "one from whom a message from God springs forth or one to whom anything is secretly communicated." Hence, the general term for prophet was one upon whom the Spirit of God rested.[78]

The first encounter between God and the prophet occurs when the word of the

---

[76] Amos 3:7

[77] Huehnergard, John, *On the Etymology and Meaning of Hebrew nābî.* Harvard University (1999). Retrieved from http://www.academia.edu/234681/1999_On_the_Etymology_and_Meaning_of_Hebrew_nabi_.

[78] Numbers 11:17 and 29

♦ ♦ ♦

Chapter 5—How to Know If You Are Called to the Office of the Prophet
The Office of the Prophet

Lord comes to him. The phrase "the word of the Lord came"[79] is prevalent throughout the Old Testament. This phrase signifies that God is revealing Himself to His servant the prophet. Once the prophet *sees* the word of God, thenceforth he is able to *speak* the will of God.[80] Habakkuk's discourse with God in **Habakkuk 2:1-3**, is a great illustration:

> ***I will stand upon my watch, and set me upon the tower, and will watch to see what he will say unto me, and what I shall answer when I am reproved.***

Here, Habakkuk declares that he will watch for (or wait to gaze upon) the word of the

---

[79] Genesis 15:1; 1 Samuel 15:10; 1 Kings 6:11; 1 Kings 17:2; Isaiah 38:4; Jeremiah 1:4; Ezekiel 3:16; Jonah 1:1, Zechariah 4:8 *passim*.

[80] Habakkuk 2:1-3

♦   ♦   ♦

Chapter 5—How to Know If You Are Called to the Office of the Prophet
The Office of the Prophet

Lord. And as he watches for the word of the Lord, or as the word of the Lord comes to him, he will then be able to see and speak the will of God. (*See also* **1 Samuel 9:27**)

Another example is the child Samuel whose mother Hannah brought him to serve in the temple under the mentorship of Eli the priest.[81] In a state of slumber, the Lord spoke to—or, the word of the Lord came to—Samuel. Aware that Samuel was unskilled and did not know God, Eli instructed the young prophet that when God came to him again, he should respond, ***"Speak, LORD; for thy servant heareth."***

What we know about Samuel from the text:

1. Samuel did not yet know the Lord. **(1 Samuel 3:7)**

---

[81] 1 Samuel 3

♦　　♦　　♦

Chapter 5—How to Know If You Are Called to the Office of the Prophet
The Office of the Prophet

> 2. Samuel served in the house of God, but did not know the God of the house. **(1 Samuel 3:7)**
>
> 3. Samuel had not yet experienced the commerce of God as an exchange in his heart. **(1 Samuel 3:10)**
>
> 4. Samuel was unable to discern the word of the Lord when it came to him because of the chaos of the house where he dwelt.

Samuel's response was the acknowledgement of his calling. It was at that moment that Samuel entered beyond the veil and a bill of exchange was made between Samuel and God. The Lord anointed Samuel as the prophetic voice in Israel—a voice that caused the ears of all of

♦ ♦ ♦

Chapter 5—How to Know If You Are Called to the Office of the Prophet
The Office of the Prophet

Israel to tingle.[82] This was monumental because at that time, the word of the Lord was precious because ***there was no open vision***.[83]

Samuel's first assignment was not to build a great edifice or become the temple successor to Eli. Samuel's first assignment was not pleasant. He was to prophesy to the one who had provided him counsel and guidance, Eli. The eternal and polarizing nature of his message was burdensome and Samuel was fearful and reluctant to reveal the message. However, Eli pressed Samuel to share because he feared God and he understood the magnitude of needing to hear a word from God—even if it was shattering and even if it was for him. So Samuel declared the counsel of God and withheld nothing. Because of the iniquity and vile

---

[82] 1 Samuel 3:11

[83] 1 Samuel 3:1

Chapter 5—How to Know If You Are Called to the Office of the Prophet
The Office of the Prophet

immorality of his sons and their utter contempt for the proper preparation of the offerings to Jehovah by the people, God declared that He would *never ever again* receive an offering or atoning sacrifice from this family! The Bible says ***"And Samuel grew, and the LORD was with him, and did let none of his words fall to the ground."*** [84] From that time forward, God elevated Samuel as both prophet and judge (one of the last judges) unto the nation of Israel.

As you study, you will learn that God reared many other prophets in the Bible—*from* Abraham in the Old Testament *to* John the Baptist in the New Testament—to confront those closest to them. That is why in Chapter 4, I discuss the necessity of the prophet being prepared to suffer rejection. Although rejection is painful, it is especially and remarkably more painful

---

[84] 1 Samuel 3:19

♦ ♦ ♦

Chapter 5—How to Know If You Are Called to the Office of the Prophet
The Office of the Prophet

from those who are dearest to us. But there is tremendous satisfaction in doing the will of God at all costs. When the prophet delights in and finds pleasure in doing God's will, he will find great satisfaction, even when rejected. ***Jesus saith unto them, My meat is to do the will of him that sent me, and to finish his work.*** **(St. John 4:34)**

It is also easy to confuse the gift of exhortation with the prophetic calling. The Greek word for exhort is *"parakaleō,"* which means to call to one's side, to admonish, to encourage, and to strengthen.[85] One who exhorts tends to respond to the reaction they receive from their audience. They need someone to agree with them or to come along side of them. However, the prophet must prepare to face unusually harsh

---

[85] Greek Dictionary (Lexicon-Concordance). Retrieved from http://lexiconcordance.com/greek/3870.html.

Chapter 5—How to Know If You Are Called to the Office of the Prophet
The Office of the Prophet

persecution, even death threats.[86] Those with a weak stomach for the battle are not called to the office of the prophet.

A prophet's job is to cry aloud and spare not[87]—even when no one stands in agreement with them. God equips the prophet to stand alone. This does not mean that they do not need others; it means that God has uniquely prepared and outfitted the prophet with the proper mental toughness to survive alone in the wilderness.

This also does not mean that the prophet is super human. The prophet deals with the same emotions as everyone else—depression, disillusionment, frustration, fear, and yes, even loneliness. Nevertheless, the prophet must speak the word of the Lord, even when it means he will suffer in the

---

[86] Jeremiah 1:19; Jeremiah 11:21

[87] Isaiah 58:1

♦ ♦ ♦

Chapter 5—How to Know If You Are Called to the Office of the Prophet
The Office of the Prophet

drought. The prophet must eat the bitter with the sweet, just like Jeremiah in the Old Testament and like John the Baptist in the New Testament.[88]

Now is a good time for you to pray and ask God for guidance. Next, pause and reflect upon the following questions, all of which serve a purpose of helping you to recognize if you have a calling to the office of the prophet:

1. Do I need others to be in agreement with what I am saying?

2. Am I willing to stand alone for the sake of the word that God has given me?

---

[88] Ezekiel 3:3; St. Matthew 3:4

♦ ♦ ♦

Chapter 5—How to Know If You Are Called to the Office of the Prophet
The Office of the Prophet

3. Does my life need to be perfect before I can speak the word of the Lord?

4. Do I allow what others say or think about me to keep me from doing God's will?

5. Am I intimidated by the position, class, or status of others?

6. Have I dealt with my own issues (flesh) and perceptions?

Once you challenge yourself in these areas of your life, perhaps you can then determine if you are called to the office of the prophet.

A prophet sees things in black and white; there are no gray areas. While on one hand, this is a tremendous characteristic, on the other hand, it can be detrimental. Because there are no grey areas, the prophet

♦ ♦ ♦

Chapter 5—How to Know If You Are Called to the Office of the Prophet
The Office of the Prophet

may begin to believe he is right and that he is more important than others. He may become quick to judge others more harshly than he does himself and will hold others to a higher standard than he does himself. The danger is when the prophet is slow to repent of his own wrong behaviors or his mistaken and erroneous thoughts, attitudes and opinions.

When the prophet of God functions at a level less than God's divine will, it is often attributed to the lack of an acknowledgement and confession by the prophet of his own humanity and capacity to make mistakes. He will soon find that his prophetic effectiveness is crippled.

It is of great benefit for the prophet to establish a relationship with a mature apostle to avoid becoming his own worst enemy. Prophets who cannot discern between truth and compassion are crippled

Chapter 5—How to Know If You Are Called to the Office of the Prophet
The Office of the Prophet

by their own perceptions. A mature apostle will advise and guide the prophet through the process of dealing with any unresolved personal issues before speaking to God's people.

If you are called to the office of the prophet, you must understand and develop the following three abilities:

1. <u>Hindsight</u>: The definition of hindsight is the "perception of the nature and demands of an event *after* it has happened."[89] Could have, should have, would have—we have all felt like this after evaluating some of our life decisions. Unfortunately, many prophets fail to learn from their mistakes or from the mistakes of others, and continue repeating certain patterns. The practice of repeating the same

---

[89] "Hindsight," *Webster's Third New International Dictionary of the English Language*, unabridged. Merriam-Webster, Inc. (1993),

Chapter 5—How to Know If You Are Called to the Office of the Prophet
The Office of the Prophet

thing over and over but expecting different results is insanity. The prophet of God should be dynamically confident in his assurance that God is with him and that God speaks to him. However, I must caution that if he is not prayerful, the prophet can become overconfident and arrogant in exercising his gift. The prophet must know, without any doubt, that he is hearing God's voice. The wise prophet will not speak his own thoughts or operate from a place of conceit.[90] Retrospectively, the prophet will have to repent when he allows his words to fall to the ground and when he utters his own thoughts.[91] Samuel was renowned as being a true prophet of God because his prophecies came to pass.

2. <u>Insight</u>: Developing proficiency in discernment is challenging for many

---

[90] Deuteronomy 18:22

[91] Lamentations 2:14; Jeremiah 14:14

♦ ♦ ♦

Chapter 5—How to Know If You Are Called to the Office of the Prophet
The Office of the Prophet

prophets. Insight is "the power or act of seeing into a situation or into oneself; discernment, penetration, understanding; the act or fact of apprehending the inner nature of things or of seeing intuitively; clear and immediate understanding."[92] It takes work, but the prophet must develop his "inner sight" and his "mental vision." The ability to "see things in the Spirit" provides significant confirmation that a person has been called to the office of the prophet. What does it mean to "see things in the spirit?" As a person (any person and not necessarily just a prophet) begins to speak God's message, God begins to download spiritual vision as an illustration of a picture in the mind's eye. This visual and graphic illustration reinforces the words that are being said. The prophet can hear one word and immediately the spirit begins to release revelation

---

[92] "Insight," *Webster's Third New International Dictionary of the English Language*, unabridged. Merriam-Webster, Inc. (1993).

◆ ◆ ◆

Chapter 5—How to Know If You Are Called to the Office of the Prophet
The Office of the Prophet

(message received from God). It is in that precise moment that the prophet must be obedient and speak what the Lord is saying. It should be understood that this does not mean randomly speaking out of turn or blurting out what one is hearing from the Lord. Doing so causes chaos and disorder, and God is not the author of confusion.[93]

3. <u>Foresight</u>: That foresight is better than hindsight is axiomatic. Guidance from apostolic headship is fundamental to the prophet as he develops foresight and discernment. Consistency and competence in decision-making are strong indicators of good foresight. The prophet must exercise patience and be very sure before making decisions. Each decision must be tested and tried to ensure that it has been weighed in the bosom of God before he goes forth to

---

[93] 1 Corinthians 14:33

♦ ♦ ♦

Chapter 5—How to Know If You Are Called to the Office of the Prophet
The Office of the Prophet

speak a word.[94] If the prophet takes heed, then when he speaks, he will move with the surety and protection of God.

During the foundational stages of prophetic development, a prophet receives only brief flashes of divine insight from the realm of the spirit. This stage can be compared to the shutter on the lens of a camera. The purpose of the shutter is to expose or allow light to pass through for a specific and determined period of time (referred to as "exposure time"). As the prophet continues to cultivate his gift and mature in his experience, he develops the ability to gaze through the prophetic lens into the realm of the spirit for longer periods of time. God grants the mature prophet longer exposure and greater divine insight into His mysteries.

---

[94] 1 John 4:1

♦ ♦ ♦

Chapter 5—How to Know If You Are Called to the Office of the Prophet
The Office of the Prophet

In many cases throughout history, the prophetic word released by God to the prophet was not lengthy. Therefore, it was uncommon for a prophet to recite lengthy prophetic discourses. When the prophet of God learns to look into the realm of the spirit to see what the Lord is saying, he will be satisfied with all that God grants him. He will be obedient to release the message, even if brief. The length of a message does not determine the power of the message.

Rarely does God provide every minuscule detail of a prophetic word to the prophet. If you are a person who cannot tolerate being "inconvenienced" by the word of the Lord, and who wants to know every detail before you speak, one of two things is taking place: (1) You are being inspired prophetically but need to mature; or (2) you simply are not called to the office of the prophet. The prophet recognizes when God is speaking. For example, "The word of the

♦　　♦　　♦

Chapter 5—How to Know If You Are Called to the Office of the Prophet
The Office of the Prophet

Lord came unto ...."[95] Once the messenger recognizes it is the Lord, he begins to speak the word of the Lord.[96]

With the exception of Jesus, you do not see any example of a prophet giving a long and detailed speech. The prophets only know in part, and prophesy in part.[97] Oftentimes, they do not realize or understand the full and complete revelation. For example, when Elijah spoke a word to Ahab from the Lord,[98] perhaps he did not realize the full ramifications of the word he spoke. He possibly did not fully realize that he too would experience heartache and would endure tribulations (drought and

---

[95] Genesis 15:1, Numbers 11:23, Numbers 23:16, Isaiah 22:14

[96] St. Mark 13:11

[97] 1 Corinthians 13:9

[98] 1 Kings 17:1

Chapter 5—How to Know If You Are Called to the Office of the Prophet
The Office of the Prophet

famine, a death threat, depression, and suicidal thoughts) as a result of that word.[99]

Because the words spoken by the prophet have the potential to change the atmosphere and the natural elements, a true prophet cares nothing about titles or positions, or about the world's systems. None of these things will satisfy the prophet because he realizes it is all about God! A true prophet gains satisfaction only by doing the will of God.

When a prophetic voice has been bestowed in the life of a prophet, he is recognized as a leader and will teach others in the prophetic. All others who hear the voice of the prophet are warned to either repent, or else fall under the wrath of God.[100] When someone tells you they are a

---

[99] 1 Kings 17 and 18

[100] 2 Chronicles 36:16

♦ ♦ ♦

Chapter 5—How to Know If You Are Called to the Office of the Prophet
The Office of the Prophet

prophet, beware of controlling spirits. Discernment from the Holy Spirit will confirm and convict those who are called to the office of the prophet.

The Lord does not want you to be discouraged. ***"For promotion cometh neither from the east, nor from the west, nor from the south. But God is the judge: he putteth down one, and setteth up another."*** **(Psalms 75:6-7)** If God has called you to be a prophetic voice in the earth, you must accept that it is neither your voice nor your words, but it is the voice of God that speaks through you.

Finally, you will know that you have been called to the office of the prophet if you possess two specific attributes. The first attribute is humility. Without modesty, meekness and an unassuming character, a prophet will undoubtedly make a mess. When that happens, God has to deal with the

♦ ♦ ♦

Chapter 5—How to Know If You Are Called to the Office of the Prophet
The Office of the Prophet

prophet in a way that brings about humility—that process can involve a lot of heartache. ***"But he giveth more grace. Wherefore he saith, God resisteth the proud, but giveth grace unto the humble."*** (**James 4:6**) It is this grace that is given by God through Jesus Christ that enables us to operate according to His design and according to His purpose.[101]

    The second attribute, of equal importance, is love. If love is not the motivating factor in all that we say or do, the gift of God will never be perfected. The gift of God is fully realized in a heart filled with love. The failure to understand this important attribute will cause the gift to eventually fade away. The heart without love is compared to the wandering stars mentioned in **Jude 13**. Why the use of the term wandering stars? Without love,

---

[101] 1 Peter 5:5, Ephesians 4:7

Chapter 5—How to Know If You Are Called to the Office of the Prophet
The Office of the Prophet

prophets will seek only the next big engagement, the next big conference, or the next big opportunity to make a name for themselves. Everything they do is all about them and consequently, they fail to make meaningful relationships that require accountability or a covenant. Without love they are without fruit, twice dead, plucked up at the root.[102] It is truly sad when we meet some of the most talented people we will ever meet, only to discover that they have not learned the two most important things in life: humility and love. This lesson can only be taught in the context of relationship. When relationship is right and the heart of the prophet is right, the heavens are opened and he is given access to divine revelation.

Every gift of God must consistently be filtered through love. If this crucial

---

[102] Jude 1:12

Chapter 5—How to Know If You Are Called to the Office of the Prophet
The Office of the Prophet

filtering process does not take place in the heart of the prophet, the purpose of the gift will never be achieved or come to fruition.

Many well-intentioned prophets start out with a good heart and a mind to do the will of God, but in the end they lack humility and love. This is illustrated by the refusal to cohabitate and fellowship with the body of believers. They begin to cut themselves off and refuse to submit to authority. While they may appear to be in submission, in reality, they have an arranged relationship. They may appear to be in covenant, but in truth, they are not. The metric to gauge this is their checkbook. The refusal to submit to headship is more often than not due to the influence of the spirit of Jezebel. The spirit of Jezebel is so threatened by the prophetic voice of God, that when a person is called to the office of the prophet, the first battle they must defeat is the stronghold of Jezebel.

♦ ♦ ♦

Chapter 5—How to Know If You Are Called to the Office of the Prophet
The Office of the Prophet

The name "Jezebel" means "non-cohabitant." The spirit of Jezebel is not gender specific. This spirit will cause the young and gifted prophet to go it alone. Once alone, the spirit of Jezebel will release the rage and anger of all of Hell against the prophetic. This spirit will drive the prophet to wish for his life to be ended. The spirit of Jezebel is intent on snuffing out the prophetic voice in the land, because it recognizes its demise has always been, and always will be, through the voice of the prophet of God.

No one can truly love God if they do not love His people who are made in His image. No one can say they are humble if they do not submit to authority. Love is proven by the ability to work with imperfect people. Although we are imperfect, God so loved us and gave Himself for us.[103] If you

---

[103] St. John 3:16

Chapter 5—How to Know If You Are Called to the Office of the Prophet
The Office of the Prophet

are called to the office of the prophet and want the gift to flow as intended by God, you must exhibit humility and love when dealing with God's people.

My Prophetic Pathway

Shortly after my call to ministry, I flew to my hometown of Lansing, Michigan. My grandmother, the late Fellersea Williams (a pastor in the Original Church of God), my mother, Pastor Geraldine Richardson, and I attended a prayer meeting. Excited about my newfound walk with Jesus, I was on fire for the Lord! (There was a time in my life when I would not in a million years have believed that I would be praising God at church with both my mother and grandmother ... on a Friday night!)

That night during an awesome time of worship, the Lord inhabited the room and rested upon each of us. The weight of His glory was so tangible that all I could do in His presence was weep uncontrollably. My grandmother was sitting and praying, my mother was sitting nearby, and I was laid out on the altar. All I remember hearing was the Lord saying "Will you go for me?" In that moment I made a life-changing

♦ ♦ ♦

Chapter 5—How to Know If You Are Called to the Office of the Prophet
The Office of the Prophet

decision and responded, "Yes Lord, yes Lord, I will go for you." In that moment of clarity I received confirmation and validation from God that indeed I was called. I no longer had to question my kingdom position.

Growing up I remembered hearing the term "filled with the Holy Ghost," an expression often used in Pentecostal churches and by a large majority of Christians. I felt as though the Lord was whipping and beating me into shape. The righteousness of God was transforming my heart so that I would run for Him for the rest of my days! It was there at that tiny house church that I fully surrendered my life to the call of God. That was my breakthrough moment—each prophet will have his own different and personal experience.

One day a church mother laid hands on me and began to ask the Lord to unlock His word in my mind. Not long afterwards, the Lord began to supernaturally drop revelation into my heart. I no longer merely read the words contained on the pages of the Bible, because as God began to transform me, the words and verses that I read literally came alive. God gave me an insatiable

♦ ♦ ♦

Chapter 5—How to Know If You Are Called to the Office of the Prophet
The Office of the Prophet

> appetite for His word. Thankfully, I have maintained that hunger and thirst for God.
>
> Until you have had a personal encounter with the living God, you will never fully understand or comprehend the divine and glorious nature of my testimony. Beyond a shadow of a doubt, I know that I am a servant of the living God and am unapologetically sold out to do His will.

Questions *(Provide scripture references where applicable)*:

1. What are the requisites of one who is called to the office of the prophet?

2. If asked, are you able to fully articulate with conviction and certainty your calling to the prophetic?

3. What characteristics must a prophet maintain to receive continual and

Chapter 5—How to Know If You Are Called to the Office of the Prophet
The Office of the Prophet

    complete access to the prophetic rhythms of God?

4. What metrics have you personally applied to your life in determining that you are called to the office of the prophet?

5. Can you identify with any of the prophetic experiences mentioned **Numbers 12:6**, **Numbers 24:4**, **Numbers 24:16**, or **Daniel 10:17**?

♦ ♦ ♦

Chapter 5—How to Know If You Are Called to the Office of the Prophet
The Office of the Prophet

_____

_____

_____

_____

_____

_____

♦ ♦ ♦

THE OFFICE OF THE PROPHET

CHAPTER 6

HOW TO DEVELOP THIS GIFT

Now that the prophet is sure of his election and his calling, it is time to develop his gift with great care and concern. The gift must be cherished by the one who carries it. It must be nourished—not worshipped—but fostered and fed to develop into what God wants.

You do not have to become weird or strange because you have a gift from God—we already are a peculiar people.[104] However, the nature of the gift will cause you to stand out even more (without any assistance from you).

In Chapter 4, we briefly mentioned the Old Testament schools of the prophets. It

---

[104] 1 Peter 2:9

Chapter 6— How to Develop This Gift
The Office of the Prophet

was in that scholarly setting that the prophets fellowshipped one with the other for the purpose of developing their God-given gifts. They shared a common bond; they knew what God was saying in the earth and they were given keys to unlock the deep mysteries of God.[105] But they needed to establish relationship with one another. To properly develop this gift, it is necessary to seek true prophets and to develop relationships with them. It is also important to study their lives, without being intrusive, to glean from them the essence of what it means to be called of God into the prophetic.

I want to share this principle found in **1 Corinthians 14:29-32**:

> ***Let the prophets speak two or three, and let the other***

---

[105] 1 Corinthians 2:10

Chapter 6— How to Develop This Gift
The Office of the Prophet

> ***judge. If any thing be revealed to another that sitteth by, let the first hold his peace. For ye may all prophesy one by one, that all may learn, and all may be comforted. And the spirits of the prophets are subject to the prophets.***

Paul instructed the church at Corinth that if one prophet spoke and God revealed anything to the other prophets around, let the one keep silent, and let the others speak and judge. He says this so that they all can prophesy. We read in Chapter 1 that in the New Testament, the testimony of Jesus Christ is the spirit of prophecy. Therefore, when a word is spoken in the church (the *ecclesia*) or at a gathering and assembly of the saints:

1. Revelation is anticipated;

♦ ♦ ♦

Chapter 6— How to Develop This Gift
The Office of the Prophet

2. Revelation is released into the atmosphere;

3. The spirit of the prophet is subject to the prophets;

4. The body is edified; and

5. A word is decreed concerning order or influence on the earth, and reveals the Kingdom of God.

All of these attributes concerning prophecy work together and no single principle should become dogma.

We now understand that to properly develop this gift, it is essential that the prophet foster relationship with a body of believers to judge what is said so that the body of Christ is edified. Remember that

Chapter 6— How to Develop This Gift
The Office of the Prophet

today's assignment for the prophetic voice is still to edify the body of Christ.[106]

Before moving forward, I want to share a word of caution: Just because you *know* a person who is a prophet, does not necessarily mean you should *be in relationship* with that particular prophet. Seek God and His wisdom concerning who He has ordained to speak into your life and to instruct you in developing your gift. The Bible provides an Old Testament example of entrusting this gift to the wrong person. A young prophet, on divine assignment from God, journeyed to the city of Bethel and met an older prophet. The older prophet lied, tricked, and deceived the young man, influencing him to disobey God. Unfortunately, the consequences of his disobedience were fatal.[107] This is a perfect

---

[106] 1 Corinthians 14:3

[107] 1 Kings 13:24

Chapter 6— How to Develop This Gift
The Office of the Prophet

example of the Jezebel spirit in action and operating across gender lines!

The lesson to be learned from this example: Always obey God. Even though someone tells you he has heard from God, it is wise to do only what God has instructed. Never assume that God has changed His mind. I honestly cannot fully comprehend why God allowed this older prophet to lie to the man of God. One thing is certain: God had already spoken to the young prophet and gave him specific instructions to neither lodge with anyone nor to eat or drink. God instructed him to return home and to not deviate from His command. His failure to obey God's orders tragically cost him his life. Although the older prophet lied to the younger prophet, God still showed him the demise and destruction of the man of God. One crucial point to note: an older and more seasoned person in the prophetic gifting can teach you some things; however, the lesson

Chapter 6— How to Develop This Gift
The Office of the Prophet

may cost more than you can afford to pay. Another lesson here—it is imperative for the prophet to develop and cultivate discernment.

Prayer and fasting is the discipline of the prophet—the prophet of God lives a fasted lifestyle and continuously seeks God's presence and His will. The prophet must take protective measures to safeguard the gift that God has entrusted to him. He must remain in a defensive posture to avoid being caught off-guard by the surrounding environment and to avoid the temptation to please everyone.

After Daniel was taken into Babylonian captivity in BC 606 at the age of fourteen, he immediately purposed in his heart that he would not defile himself with the king's diet and that he would not acquiesce to the customs of the

Chapter 6— How to Develop This Gift
The Office of the Prophet

Babylonians.[108] He would not bring displeasure to His God. This reminds me of the popular phrases: "You are what you eat" and "tell me what you eat, and I will tell you what you are." Daniel, accustomed to a fasted lifestyle, quickly recognized the underlying scheme of the king of Babylonia. His scheme—feed them his tainted diet and get them to think the thoughts of the gods of Babylon. The result of living a fasted life is that Daniel and his contemporaries—Hananiah, Mishael and Azariah—were healthier, stronger, wiser, and more skilled than anyone else in Nebuchadnezzar's realm.[109]

Moreover, Daniel had a remarkable and disciplined prayer life. He meticulously prayed three times a day before and after Babylonian captivity—he did not break this

---

[108] Daniel 1:8

[109] Daniel 1:20

Chapter 6— How to Develop This Gift
The Office of the Prophet

pattern of prayer even in prison.[110] Prayer in the life of the prophet is an intentional and major commitment. I promise you that if you begin your prophetic journey with prayer, consecration, and personal devotion, you will develop the brokenness and humility that God desires in the hearts of his prophets.

The prophet will soon discover that prayer is not a monologue or lecture to God. It is not a complaint about all that is wrong. Prayer is not a list of things needed from God, as though He does not know the things you have need of or that He needs to be informed about your life. **St. Matthew 6:8** says, ***"Be not ye therefore like unto them: for your Father knoweth what things ye have need of, before ye ask him."*** The prophet of God will learn that prayer is a dialogue with God and is a beautiful time of

---

[110] Daniel 6:10

Chapter 6— How to Develop This Gift
The Office of the Prophet

communion with your Creator—He who will provide you with divine insight concerning the prophetic visions of heaven.

To the believer prayer is the umbilical cord (or birth cord), the channel through which God Almighty provides us with the spiritually-rich nutrients needed to sustain us in the earth realm. As the prophet steals away to his prayer chamber, he rests in the presence of God and awaits instructions from Elohim, according to **Romans 8:26:** ***"Likewise the Spirit also helpeth our infirmities: for we know not what we should pray for as we ought: but the Spirit itself maketh intercession for us with groanings which cannot be uttered."*** The prophet of God recognizes that he must linger in the presence of God so that the glory of God is released. The prophet begins to develop a yearning and waits until he receives insight into the heart of God.

♦ ♦ ♦

Chapter 6— How to Develop This Gift
The Office of the Prophet

After residing in the divine presence of God through prayer, the heart of the prophet of God is transformed and he departs having had a "burning bush" encounter![111] One cannot simply walk away from God's Shekinah presence and not be changed.

When you have been in God's presence you are transformed by His love, by His glory, and by His enlightenment! You depart His presence with His favor bestowed into your life.

Elijah and John the Baptist provide two more examples of a fasted lifestyle. God sent Elijah to several places where a sacrifice of fasting was required: at the brook Cherith on the east side of the Jordan, and at Beersheba where an angel fed him a meal that would provide sustenance and

---

[111] Exodus 3:2

Chapter 6— How to Develop This Gift
The Office of the Prophet

strength to fast—40 days and 40 nights.[112] John the Baptist ate locusts and wild honey in the wilderness of Judea.[113] The calling of John the Baptist was epic and monumental: to prepare the way of the Lord.[114] The burden of this historic role required a continual fasted life. It was of great benefit to John that he surrendered to a clean, wholesome, and nutritional diet.

As Jesus sent forth the seventy before him into every city and place, he instructed them to eat whatever was set before them.[115] As prophetic messengers, they were to live simple lives and be thankful for the provisions they would receive from others. A fasted life produces a consecrated walk.

---

[112] 1 Kings 19:5-8

[113] St. Matthew 3:4

[114] Isaiah 40:1-4

[115] St. Luke 10:1-8

♦ ♦ ♦

Chapter 6— How to Develop This Gift
The Office of the Prophet

The prophet is responsible for careful stewardship of his gift. He must listen to and be guided by the voice of God through the leading of the Holy Ghost continually—24 hours a day, seven days a week. This will allow the prophet to be weaned off milk and able to digest the meat of the word of righteousness.[116]

A prophet is entrusted to speak the divine oracles of God and there is no margin for error. Once again, I believe this explains the need for a school of the prophets in the Old Testament. The prophets needed a place where they could exercise and train for the perfecting of their gifts. Repetition is one of the best ways to develop any gift; the more you practice, the more proficient you become. If you feel that you have a prophetic anointing and that you are called

---

[116] Hebrews 5:13-14

Chapter 6— How to Develop This Gift
The Office of the Prophet

by God, it will come forth when you are around other prophets.

There are particular environments where the prophetic gift is released; one of those environments is during heavy worship.[117] It is during worship when the prophetic flow is released that the revelation of Jesus is received ... the testimony of Jesus. One of the most tremendous and indispensable requisites of the prophet is the amount of quality worship time spent with God—alone. The prophetic calling requires many personal sacrifices, including times of isolation and loneliness. In many instances, although the prophet is surrounded by crowds or in a room full of family and friends, there is a feeling of loneliness. Why is the prophet required to make such sacrifices? It is because the hand of the Lord resides in the life of the one called, and His

---

[117] 2 Kings 3:15

Chapter 6— How to Develop This Gift
The Office of the Prophet

spirit urges them to a higher place. The prophet responds with a desire and yearning for more of God because he understands that ***in thy presence is fulness of joy!***[118] He understands that he can only find complete satisfaction in the presence of the Lord!

The prophet does not have the luxury of depending upon others to fulfill what only God can fulfill. The prophet looks to God to validate and encourage him. Clearly, the prophet who is unable to commune with God when no one else is around has some more growing to do and another level of maturity to reach. It is during those intimate times of closeness with God that He literally becomes a friend. Now God is able to disclose His revelation to His servant along with His instructions and marching orders!

---

[118] Psalms 16:11

♦ ♦ ♦

Chapter 6— How to Develop This Gift
The Office of the Prophet

I wish to impart a few final thoughts concerning the development of the prophetic gift. The prophet must become a slave—a slave to the Word of God. You must saturate and inundate your mind with God's Word every waking moment of your life. The Word of God must be your meat and drink morning, noon, and night. God told me, "If you read, you will bleed; if you pray, you will stay; and if you fast, you will last."

The true servant of the Lord recognizes his position as a bondservant of the Lord.[119] The bondservant does not propagate his own agenda and he does not advance his own vision. He becomes detached from what he wants to do. He becomes blind and deaf to his own will. His objective is to do the will of God. A shift in

---

[119] Isaiah 42:19-20

Chapter 6— How to Develop This Gift
The Office of the Prophet

his attitude takes place and like Jesus, he desires only to do the will of his Father.[120]

Prayer and supplication will help to balance the behavior of the prophet even as it relates to his relationships and interactions with others. The prophet of God must seek God for compassion and understanding of the human condition. Paul recognized that we are all fallible and subject to sin. He considered that even as he preached to others, it was conceivable that he could fall from grace.[121] The prophet should forever preserve compassion in his heart, for without it he will not be as effective in the lives of others.

Through a vivid and life-altering experience, the Prophet Ezekiel learned compassion for humanity. Ezekiel was

---

[120] St. John 5:30

[121] 1 Corinthians 9:27

Chapter 6— How to Develop This Gift
The Office of the Prophet

among approximately 10,000 Jews displaced from their homes and exiled from Judah. They were taken to Tel-Abib in Babylon.

Whatever Ezekiel witnessed with his own eyes at Tel-Abib was indescribable and unspeakable because Ezekiel said ***"I sat where they sat, and remained there astonished among them seven days."***[122] *Beginning* with the first recorded war engaged by the four Mesopotamian kings of the east against the kings of Sodom and Gomorrah *to* present-day military engagements and conflicts, history is replete with a catalog of the brutalities of war. When nations and people war against each other, no one wins and the loss of human life is inestimable. It is a sad commentary that in every war there are those who become morally diminished; they reduce themselves to severely persecuting and harming others.

---

[122] Ezekiel 3:15

Chapter 6— How to Develop This Gift
The Office of the Prophet

Snatched and ripped away from all that was familiar and safe and taken captive to a foreign land was catastrophic and heartbreaking beyond human comprehension. Ezekiel says that as he sat among his compatriots, he was *astonished*. Even God's mouthpiece could only open his mouth in silence—for seven days he remained vocally paralyzed.

Tel-Abib indelibly changed Ezekiel's heart forever. Although Ezekiel prophesied against the leaders for their idolatry, when eventually imprisoned by the Babylonians, he felt affinity for their suffering. Ezekiel developed a heart of compassion for his fellow Jews in their time of suffering. When the prophet of God feels indebted to Christ and is thankful for His grace and mercy, he will demonstrate compassion as he deals with the souls of men.

♦   ♦   ♦

Chapter 6— How to Develop This Gift
The Office of the Prophet

It may be necessary to read and reread this chapter many times to comprehend the concepts of how to develop your gift. You must accept the truths contained herein as relevant and necessary for your life. You must seek God to know if this is the life He has called you to.

> **My Prophetic Pathway**
>
> Returning to Denver, I placed myself under the tutelage of Bishop Holiman, an awesome man of God anointed to help develop the gift within others. He teaches sound doctrine from the word of God and his mentorship still helps me to understand the necessity of being submitted to apostolic headship. After several years of growing in faith and exercising my prophetic gift, it became obvious to all who knew me that the Lord's hand was on me.
>
> One Sunday morning I invited my younger brother to come to church. As Bishop Holiman was preaching, a sudden disruption was taking place in the midst of the congregation. Whatever was happening had become such a distraction that it was obvious to Bishop Holiman and the other ministers that service

♦ ♦ ♦

Chapter 6— How to Develop This Gift
The Office of the Prophet

needed to come to a halt. An elderly gentleman was unresponsive and as his daughter frantically waved and cried out for help, a nurse and several others came to aid her.

I was disappointed that the service had come to a screeching stop because I wanted my brother to get saved! I was thinking that we do not have time for any drama because (1) my brother needed to see Jesus and (2) Bishop Holiman needed to give the altar call. I was determined that my brother would come to Jesus that day! But the Lord had another plan. The elderly gentleman was not breathing, he had no pulse, and he was as white as a sheet. He had passed away during the service. I thought what in the world is this all about? Being the typical goal-oriented person that I am, my only thought was to manage this inconvenience and get back to church as usual.

For about 20 minutes, we checked his pulse and breathing, but he had no pulse and he was not breathing. Someone had already called 911 and we could hear the sirens. I suggested that we remove him from the congregation so that we could calm everyone and bring order to the scene. But no one

♦ ♦ ♦

Chapter 6— How to Develop This Gift
The Office of the Prophet

> wanted to touch a dead man.
>
> Suddenly I felt boldness from God that I had not ever before experienced. I picked up the gentleman and began walking down the middle aisle and out of the sanctuary. Before I reached the door, I heard the voice of God saying, "Call on the name of Jesus!" I obeyed and began to say Jesus, Jesus, Jesus! While calling on the name of Jesus, the man began to move and I heard his breath return to him. To God be the glory! I walked down the stairs and as I laid him on a table, the Lord spoke again, "You're done here; go back into service," which had resumed. That day God performed a miracle and He chose me, a young prophet, to fulfill His will. I am happy to say that my brother has since come to Christ, but not that day. What a turning point in my journey into the prophetic!

♦ ♦ ♦

Chapter 6— How to Develop This Gift
The Office of the Prophet

Questions *(Provide scripture references where applicable)*:

1. How has this chapter impacted your decision to continue in your divine calling in the prophetic?

2. What personal sacrifices have you purposely made to develop the prophetic anointing in your life?

3. Why is consecration of the utmost importance in the life of the prophet?

4. How does prayer specifically impact the development of the prophetic gift?

♦ ♦ ♦

Chapter 6— How to Develop This Gift
The Office of the Prophet

_____

_____

_____

_____

_____

_____

_____

_____

♦ ♦ ♦

THE OFFICE OF THE PROPHET

CHAPTER 7

HOW TO PROTECT THIS GIFT

Chapter 7 is very important and although some of what I will cover in this chapter has previously been addressed, please do not ignore the invaluable information to follow.

Now that you understand how to develop this gift, you must not fail to acknowledge that it is precious; you must protect and cherish it. The prophet has the power of death and life in his tongue.[123] The power of his words changes nations and the hearts of kings. Therefore, the prophet must be ever so careful not to speak in an irresponsible, careless, and reckless manner. While this is true for every believer, the one who operates within the prophetic has a

---

[123] Proverbs 18:21

Chapter 7—How to Protect This Gift
The Office of the Prophet

greater responsibility to the Word of God. God demands greater accountability from the prophet.

The most important goal for the prophet of God is to walk consistently in holiness and purity. If he fails to do this, the effectiveness of his gift will very quickly be diminished, even snuffed out. The prophet of God must not presumptuously harbor secrets or sin. The call of the prophet is to hear from the Holy One, the Ancient of Days, the Creator of all that is in the Universe, and He who is Sovereign and knows the future for eternity. Thus, the prophet must overcome the flesh and walk in purity to speak the heart of God without fear, condemnation, and shame. The office of the prophet is the highest of all callings.

One way to protect the gift is to avoid the temptation to listen to or to repeat gossip. Gossip is dangerous and extremely harmful. The Bible speaks of a talebearer as

♦ ♦ ♦

Chapter 7—How to Protect This Gift
The Office of the Prophet

one who reveals secrets.[124] Generally, the talebearer reveals secrets for the purpose of humiliating others or for self-elevation. The spirit of gossip will kill the power and influence of the prophet's words faster than almost anything else. Many times [s]atan will attempt to bring gossip to the prophet for the sake of tainting and polluting the words that proceed out of his mouth. This ploy is designed to prevent God's intended purpose in the atmosphere and to weaken the prophetic anointing. When a person brings sensational and scandalous conversation to the prophet, the prophet must instantly recognize them as messengers sent by [s]atan. Do not allow anyone to destroy your anointing by planting the seeds of gossip in your heart. You must stop them.[125] To protect the gift, the prophet must do all he can to ensure the effectiveness of

---

[124] Proverbs 11:13

[125] Proverbs 21:23

Chapter 7—How to Protect This Gift
The Office of the Prophet

his words, so that God's will in the earth is accomplished.

Here is additional insight concerning the spirit of gossip. The gift of the prophetic is often generational, and [s]atan attempts to stunt and impede the impact a particular family has in the earth. If [s]atan can infiltrate the family tree with the spirit of gossip, he knows he can hinder and delay that family's kingdom dominion and influence in the earth. Another danger in entertaining this spirit is the bad fruit it can produce: poverty and sickness. Have you ever seen an anointed and gifted prophet who is financially busted, or who has unusual amounts of sickness in his body or among his family members? Gossip will kill you, or should I say, gossip is killing you. If you have found yourself caught up by the spirit of gossip, confess it, repent, and turn away from it. Ask the Lord for forgiveness now. This prayer is for cleansing of the lips:

♦ ♦ ♦

Chapter 7—How to Protect This Gift
The Office of the Prophet

> *Dear Lord Jesus, I have given myself over to gossip. I ask for forgiveness now, in the name of the Lord Jesus Christ. I confess my sins and receive the forgiveness of sins through the blood of Jesus Christ. Please apply the coals of your holy altar and cleanse my lips, as you did for the Prophet Isaiah.[126] From this day forward, I will guard my lips and keep them from being used for gossip, and verbal destruction to the Kingdom of God.*

The next few paragraphs very well may be the most important paragraphs in this entire book; they are worthy of double consideration. Thankfully, we live in the

---

[126] Isaiah 6:6-7

Chapter 7—How to Protect This Gift
The Office of the Prophet

"information age" (also referred to as the "computer age" or the "digital age"). However, there is a "down side" to living in this age. Our minds are constantly bombarded with, and hijacked by, tremendous amounts of information from countless media sources. Some of these media sources include: advertising and broadcasting media, digital and electronic media, hypermedia, multimedia, news media, printed and published media, and recorded media, to name a few.

A recent phenomenon is the implementation of social media, which has broadened our interaction with and connection to people all over the world. This allows for worldwide circulation and distribution of information. Everyday citizens have become iReporters or citizen journalists, who reveal to the world what is happening in their neighborhoods and in their world. This information is uploaded in

♦ ♦ ♦

Chapter 7—How to Protect This Gift
The Office of the Prophet

the form of audio, videos, and photographs. All of these sources over-stimulate the mind and can be captivating, obsessive, and addictive.

One of the prevailing strategies [s]atan uses to attack the prophetic voice of God, is to abort or avoid the spoken word. [s]atan has intentionally designed a platform where the spoken word is replaced with texts, emails, chats, and tweets. These forms of written communication aid in silencing the voice of the prophet. No matter how powerful social media has or will become, it is vital that the prophet's voice is heard. The prophetic sound must never cease to be released in the earth. In order for the prophetic rhythms of heaven to be activated in the earth, the prophetic voice must be spoken.

Aristotle (384 BC–322 BC), the Greek philosopher, stated, "All men by

Chapter 7—How to Protect This Gift
The Office of the Prophet

nature desire to know."[127] While the importance of knowledge and information should not be disregarded, it is imperative that the prophet guard what enters into his spirit by way of the Internet and television, and a multitude of other media sources. This spirit of the media, another stronghold against which the prophet must guard against, is also the spirit of antichrist.

The spirit of antichrist is an ancient spirit that has resided in the earth since the fall of [s]atan after God cast him out of heaven.[128] The spirit of antichrist opposes everything that you aspire to do and everything that you are called to do in the Kingdom of God.[129]

---

[127] Wikiquote. Retrieved from http://en.wikiquote.org/wiki/Aristotle.

[128] Isaiah 14:12-14, Ezekiel 28:12-19

[129] 1 John 2:22, 1 John 4:3

♦ ♦ ♦

Chapter 7—How to Protect This Gift
The Office of the Prophet

One example of the prevalence of this ancient spirit in the earth is found in the book of Daniel, during the reign of Cyrus II (600 or 576 BC–530 BC)[130] in Persia. Cyrus was the grandson of a Mede King, ruler of the Median Empire, an ancient Iranian kingdom. Daniel (whose name means "Justice from God") set his heart to humble himself before God, and to confess his sins and the sins of the people.[131] God responded to Daniel's sincere cry and dispatched a messenger to carry a word for the people. But the Prince of Persia withstood the messenger for twenty-one days. Ultimately, Michael the archangel came and helped him to break through so that he could get to Daniel.[132] The spirit of Persia was a dark territorial spirit. The kingdom of Persia has always been at war against the prophetic.

---

[130] Also known as Cyrus the Great.

[131] Daniel 10:12

[132] Daniel 10:13

♦ ♦ ♦

Chapter 7—How to Protect This Gift
The Office of the Prophet

Just as the spirit of Persia was a dark territorial spirit, the age of the media, as we know it today, is a territorial spirit that has the potential to negatively dominate and influence thoughts, attitudes, and opinions. The prophet will inevitably lose his anointing if he allows himself to become addicted to the news and to the Internet, and who allows the data he receives to influence him more than God. The prince of the media is [s]atan, and he wants to pervert the prophetic. This evil influence hinders the pure message of God by massively inundating the mind with information, data, communications, and news on a large-scale.

Beware of spending too much time on the Internet and attacking your brain with too much information from your desktop, laptop, smart phone, iPod®, iBook®, iPhone®, iPad®,[133] etc. While these all are

---

[133] Apple.com, *Apple Trademark List*. Retrieved from http://www.apple.com/legal/trademark/appletmlist.html.

inanimate and inorganic, the prophet should guard against becoming enslaved to them. There are many who intend to proliferate and disseminate their evil agendas by constantly streaming information to you through these items. It is the information and the user behind the device that are evil.

I believe that the influence of the media and of social media can become a dangerous stronghold. This influence is deliberate. It is designed to thwart the true message of God that brings breakthrough and deliverance in the lives of His people. The adage "the pen is mightier than the sword" suggests that written communication and administrative power is a more effective tool than direct violence. But the sword of the Spirit, the spoken word of God, is inestimably and infinitely more powerful than the pen. The prophetic sound of the voice of the prophet is the greatest weapon

♦ ♦ ♦

that can be launched against the powers of darkness.

God created man in His own image and likeness and, therefore, He desires to release His mind and his thoughts in the earth. While the prophetic voice of the prophet of God will never be silenced in the earth, the prophet must diligently protect his gift.

I pray this chapter has exposed just how subtle, shrewd, and crafty [s]atan is. Prophet of God, I challenge you to give prayerful and honest consideration to the following questions:

1. As you read this chapter, were you convicted by the Holy Ghost?

2. If you miss one night of watching or viewing any type of media, do you feel a void, as though you may have missed something important?

♦ ♦ ♦

Chapter 7—How to Protect This Gift
The Office of the Prophet

3. Do you daily read the newspaper from front to back?

4. Do you spend an inordinate and excessive amount of time on the Internet viewing and reading things, or participating in games or other activities that are not wholesome?

5. Finally, do these questions make you feel anger, shame, or guilt?

If you answered <u>yes</u> to more than one of these questions, repeat the following prayer out loud. The power of this prayer will protect the gift God has given to you for His glory:

> *Father God, I thank you for trusting me with your precious gift. I am sorry for my lack of due diligence in protecting it and in being the proper steward over it. I*

♦ ♦ ♦

Chapter 7—How to Protect This Gift
The Office of the Prophet

> *confess my sins concerning the spirit of the media. With your help, I purpose in my heart to guard my eye-gate and ear-gate from worldly influences, so that I may be a purified weapon in your hands. Now sanctify me, wash me, and purify me through the blood of the Lamb, in Jesus' name. Amen.*

I believe that as you continue to meditate on this chapter, you are more determined than ever to protect your gift. I now challenge you not to read the newspaper, watch the news, or spend time on the Internet for one week. Instead, I invite you to a time of consecration, fasting, and entering into the presence of God. If you seek His face through worship, the study of His Holy Word, and prayer, I promise, my friend, that you will receive a tremendous

♦ ♦ ♦

breakthrough and a fresh anointing from the Lord!

The following scriptures will be of great benefit during this time of fasting: **Isaiah, Chapter 58; Joel, Chapter 2; Romans 12:1-3; 2 Corinthians, Chapter 6;** and **James, Chapter 3**.

My Prophetic Pathway

One Friday night after an exciting Bible study, I decided to quickly stop by the grocery store for chips and dip because I was anxious to arrive home in time to watch my favorite program. I had exchanged my former Friday night entertainment—bars and clubs—for a new Friday night entertainment, "Friday Night Frights!" One of the main characters in this series was the infamous Freddy Krueger of "Nightmare on Elm Street," and at that time I loved watching scary movies. But the Lord began to convict my heart before I reached home and said, "You are now operating on another level which is spiritual and you cannot afford to expose your spirit to the demonic." I was shocked to hear the Lord speak so clearly—it felt as though He was sitting next

♦   ♦   ♦

Chapter 7—How to Protect This Gift
The Office of the Prophet

to me in my car. I am sure you want to know was that the end of "Friday Night Frights?" The answer is yes! I obeyed the Lord and closed the door to that kind of entertainment.

The Lord dealt with me on another occasion about the deep need in my soul to satisfy my ego. The formal training I received in martial arts provided me the opportunity to compete in karate tournaments which generally convened Sunday afternoons. I lived for the excitement of winning large trophies and thrived on the applause and accolades from my fans. It was exhilarating to enter a gymnasium and see everyone stop to recognize my skill and honor my accomplishments. While some may have been humbled by and thankful for the recognition, I *needed* the thrill and validation those moments provided.

On one occasion while my father was visiting me in Denver, I was preparing to perform at such a tournament. But by the time I was ready to go, I began to feel uneasy in my spirit and did not have my usual enthusiasm. I began to hesitate as I vacillated, "I love Jesus." "I love karate." Noticing my anxiety, my father spoke these words, "If you cannot enjoy it, it is not worth having." I needed to hear

Chapter 7—How to Protect This Gift
The Office of the Prophet

> those words. The Lord used my father to bring a word of healing to my soul along with a conviction that I must make a choice. That day I made my choice: I took off my karate uniform, stayed home to enjoy my father's company, and decided to be content.
>
> But God was not yet through with me about martial arts and continued to bring me under conviction concerning my attitude and mentality in competition. To be successful and return home victorious, I had developed an attitude of indifference towards my opponent in competition and lacked compassion in my heart. I was willing to do whatever it took to win—even if it meant hurting another man—one created in the image of God. God challenged me to separate from this mindset because it stands in direct opposition to God's heart. Tough lessons, but I was truly on the road to transformation.
>
> In instructing me how to protect my gift, God required an intimate walk and He demanded sacrifice. It was now time for me to abandon the carnal and worldly, and sanctify myself unto that which is holy. I was beginning to understand that sanctification and sacrifice are foundational to

♦ ♦ ♦

Chapter 7—How to Protect This Gift
The Office of the Prophet

> protecting the gift.

Questions *(Provide scripture references where applicable)*:

1. Do you have an apostolic covering to mentor and disciple you in how to protect your gift?

2. What are tactics used by [s]atan today to distract and hinder the prophetic from being released in the earth?

3. Moving forward in your ministry, what will you implement in your daily life to safeguard and defend this high gift that God has bestowed upon you?

4. What are other inherent dangers that the prophet faces as he walks in the prophetic?

♦ ♦ ♦

Chapter 7—How to Protect This Gift
The Office of the Prophet

5. What are weapons of defense that the prophet can employ to protect his gift?

♦ ♦ ♦

Chapter 7—How to Protect This Gift
The Office of the Prophet

_____

_____

_____

_____

_____

_____

_____

♦   ♦   ♦

THE OFFICE OF THE PROPHET

CHAPTER 8

HOW TO CARRY THIS GIFT

I want to deal with the subject how to carry this gift metaphorically or symbolically, rather than from a literal viewpoint. The Bible says, *"But we have this treasure in earthen vessels, that the excellency of the power may be of God, and not of us."* **(2 Corinthians 4:7)** This scripture is the foundation of my discussion below.

As previously discussed in Chapter 5, humility is one of the greatest characteristics a leader can possess. The office of the prophet comes with a mandate to walk in humility. The greater the gift, the more humility is required. Humility comes

Chapter 8—How to Carry This Gift
The Office of the Prophet

before honor.[134] The prophet who lacks humility is a prophet destined for failure.

There is a difference between appearing to walk in humility, and actually being humble. Vain or false meekness mimics humility. Conversely, a person with the spirit of discernment sees through the mask and cloak, and recognizes the true heart. I continue to repeat the necessity of fellowship and communion among the prophets. Fellowship and the building of relationships help to develop humility in the heart of the prophet. The prophets hold each other accountable and exhort each other as it relates to walking in humility. Like Saul, the prophet of God who isolates and segregates himself from a community of prophets may be setting himself up for his demise. Throughout the Bible God reveals His character to us through relationships so that

---

[134] Proverbs 18:12

Chapter 8—How to Carry This Gift
The Office of the Prophet

we can understand the value of bonding and connecting with others.

There are some who study the Bible and their only motive is to try to figure God out. Once they have studied, they place the God of the Bible and the Bible into a box as a sign of their presumptuous belief that they have completely figured Him out. This is a first step toward developing an attitude of vain humility. Because God is transcendent and supreme, there is no "figuring Him out." David wrote about God and said ***Such knowledge is too wonderful for me; it is high, I cannot attain unto it.***[135] He recognized that he could not come to any conclusion about the supreme God of the Bible, and understood that he did not have enough imagination to ever know or understand all there is to know about God.

---

[135] Psalms 139:6

♦ ♦ ♦

Chapter 8—How to Carry This Gift
The Office of the Prophet

Isaiah asked and then answered the questions about God that have troubled man throughout the ages: ***Hast thou not known? hast thou not heard, that the everlasting God, the LORD, the Creator of the ends of the earth, fainteth not, neither is weary?*** He then answered ***there is no searching of his understanding.*** [136] In the New Testament, John concludes that ***[T]here are also many other things which Jesus did, the which, if they should be written every one, I suppose that even the world itself could not contain the books that should be written. Amen.*** [137] These wise men recognized that mankind does not have the knowledge or wisdom to form any kind of conclusive or irrefutable definition of God. All we know is what God says of Himself, I AM THAT I AM. [138]

---

[136] Isaiah 40:28

[137] St. John 21:25

[138] Exodus 3:14

♦ ♦ ♦

Chapter 8—How to Carry This Gift
The Office of the Prophet

While we cannot know all there is to know about God, to properly carry the gift, the prophet must build relationships with and interact with other prophets who carry the gift. The prophet must learn to humbly value relationships with other prophets as well as with other people.

Walking in humility means that the prophet must not take himself too seriously. A false sense of humility will cause you to not enjoy life as God intends. A false sense of humility will also cause you to believe that you are the only one who really knows God.

The prophet Elijah achieved tremendous victories and amazing conquests in his encounters with the forces of darkness and in defeating the prophets of Baal. However, he began to take himself too serious. Convinced that he was the only one

Chapter 8—How to Carry This Gift
The Office of the Prophet

who had not bowed his knee to Baal,[139] Elijah ended up hiding in a cave. He took himself so seriously that, I can imagine the Lord asking, "What are you doing here, Elijah?"[140] I have work for you to do. What are you doing down here on Self-pity Avenue, this desolate and depressed place? You decided to come here because of your lack of humility, but I did not send you here.

The Lord recognizes our frailties and will minister to us, just like He ministered to Elijah. The Lord led Elijah to a mount where He sent an enormous wind, but the Lord was not in the wind. The Lord then sent seismic activity into the atmosphere, but He was not in the earthquake. The Lord then sent a spectacular fire, but the scripture says that the Lord was not in any of these.[141]

---

[139] 1 Kings 19:10, Romans 11:3

[140] 1 Kings 19:9

[141] 1 Kings 19:11

Chapter 8—How to Carry This Gift
The Office of the Prophet

Surprisingly, the Lord was in a "still small voice." In a whisper, God spoke!

We often look for God to appear in a brilliant, spectacular, and breathtaking manner so that we can positively know that it is Him. He has already revealed to us just how awesome He is in an elaborate style:

> ***"For the invisible things of him from the creation of the world are clearly seen, being understood by the things that are made, [even] his eternal power and Godhead; so that they are without excuse …."*** **(Romans 1:20)**

He has revealed Himself to us through His word, through nature, and through his Son Jesus Christ. He also desires that we recognize Him in the simple things in life—things as simple as bouncing your

♦ ♦ ♦

Chapter 8—How to Carry This Gift
The Office of the Prophet

grandchild on your knee, taking time to watch a splendid sunrise or sunset, or simply by enjoying a walk in the park.

Through humility and by remaining small in our own eyes, we are able to recognize *Him* in the simplest revelation. I love when God whispers his desires into my ears. As long as we remain small in our own eyes, we will be fine. Genuine and authentic humility is an important key to carrying the mantel of the prophetic gift. When the prophet learns to remain transparent before God and before God's people, he stands a better chance of walking in genuine humility.

Please take my advice to avoid believing in (or reading) your own press. While it may be unintended, the danger in doing so is that the prophet can become egotistical, vain, self-serving and self-

Chapter 8—How to Carry This Gift
The Office of the Prophet

absorbed. There is no room for narcissism and self-promotion in kingdom work.

Another danger is the fine line between truth and fairytales. Fairytales and myths cause one to lose touch with reality. Truthfully, no one cares about our personal press releases because they are dealing with their own realities and life experiences. The proud and boastful prophet begins to lose touch with others and will soon lose touch with God causing God's voice to become distant. If you begin to activate the principles of this chapter in your life, you will walk in humility and you will have respect for others.

The prophet cannot properly carry this gift until he has conquered fear. Fear has torment.[142] We all have times when we must defeat this enemy of our soul—in face-

---

[142] 1 John 4:18

Chapter 8—How to Carry This Gift
The Office of the Prophet

to-face combat. When faced with this enemy, we must fight with great tenacity, so that we are not overtaken or paralyzed by fear. Fear produces doubt. When the heart is overwhelmed by doubt, the prophet will begin to question who is really speaking: Is God truly speaking or are these my words? If the enemy can cause fear to grip the heart of the prophet, he understands that the prophet will become apprehensive and afraid to proclaim what "thus saith the Lord."

Herod Antipas had John the Baptist imprisoned for speaking out against his adulterous relationship with Herodias, his brother's wife.[143] At some point, John the Baptist began to surrender to the circumstances of his solitary confinement. Do we detect fear in the mighty preacher? He began to experience fear and trepidation

---

[143] St. Luke 3:19

Chapter 8—How to Carry This Gift
The Office of the Prophet

about his conviction that Jesus was the Christ and even began to question if his preaching was in error. John sent two of his disciples to inquire of Jesus, "***Art thou he that should come, or do we look for another?***"[144] This great prophet needed assurance from Christ to overcome fear. Jesus answered:

> ***Go and shew John again those things which ye do hear and see: The blind receive their sight, and the lame walk, the lepers are cleansed, and the deaf hear, the dead are raised up, and the poor have the gospel preached to them. And blessed is he, whosoever shall not be offended in me.* (Matthew 11:4-6)**

---

[144] St. Matthew 11:3

♦ ♦ ♦

Chapter 8—How to Carry This Gift
The Office of the Prophet

Assurance from Christ was all that the prophet needed to remain courageous and steadfast. Like John the Baptist, the prophet must never cease to point beyond and away from himself. As he carries the gift, he must direct others to Jesus Christ.

Fear presents another problem for the prophet. Fear likes to torment leaders by haunting them with their past. Fear asks, "Who do you think you are?" "How dare you speak to these people?" "Did you forget that you have baggage?" Fear never lets us forget our past. One defense mechanism to counterattack fear is to recognize that fear is rooted in pride! We must be vigilant to recognize [s]atan's tactics. When he sees us gripped by fear, he uses it against us with a vengeance. It cannot be avoided—we have to face our fears. If not, we will end up in situations similar to Abraham and Elijah. Because Abraham feared for his life, he lied to Abimelech. Elijah's fear that Jezebel

♦ ♦ ♦

Chapter 8—How to Carry This Gift
The Office of the Prophet

would kill him caused him to run away and go into hiding. All liars are cowards. The Bible admonishes that the fearful and liars shall have their part in the lake which burneth with fire and brimstone.[145] The prophet must recognize that he is subject to his own personal baggage. Failure to deal with the past will cause the prophet to see through the eyes of suspicion.

[s]atan has no new tricks, just an infinite way of bringing up the same old stuff. A lack of godly discernment will get you into trouble. There are three areas employed by [s]atan to lure and tempt the believer: (1) the lust of the flesh, (2) the lust of the eyes, and (3) the pride of life.[146] Fear is directly related to the pride of life. Operating his gift through pride is one way the prophet can become gripped by fear.

---

[145] Revelation 21:8

[146] 1 John 2:16

Chapter 8—How to Carry This Gift
The Office of the Prophet

When facing a situation that could cause embarrassment, the mind will become locked and unable to discern the mind of God.

It is difficult to be embarrassed when you have no pride! Pride always precedes shame and embarrassment. ***"When pride cometh, then cometh shame: but with the lowly is wisdom."*** **(Proverbs 11:2)** That is why I recommend fasting and consecration. ***"Blessed are they which do hunger and thirst after righteousness: for they shall be filled."*** (**St. Matthew 5:6**) A person truly hungry and thirsty for God surrenders his pride, so that when the opportunity is presented, he is able to eat and drink. The hungry and thirsty person becomes transparent before God. He is not concerned about the people's perception of him, because he has no more pride. At this point in his life, the prophet simply seeks to

Chapter 8—How to Carry This Gift
The Office of the Prophet

satisfy a basic need—the need for what is godly.

[s]atan tries to project a negative mental image in the mind of the prophet by persuading him to feel shame. If [s]atan is successful, the prophet is hindered from walking in the prophetic and from fulfilling God's order for his life. In order for the prophet to flow freely in his office, he must set his face like a flint. He must become blind and deaf to what [s]atan says, and certainly to what people say.

The prophet's focus must be on Jesus; he cannot see or hear Jesus if his focus is about himself. The effective prophetic ministry is one where complete allegiance is to God—to nothing else and to no one else!

The ministry of John the Baptist was effective because he learned to emotionally

♦ ♦ ♦

Chapter 8—How to Carry This Gift
The Office of the Prophet

detach from his family and friends, and from worldly desires. He was not interested in fortune and fame or in political gain. He did not have a hidden and personal agenda. He was not interested in fancy clothing and luxurious homes. He was not consumed with an appetite for the delicacies of his time. John instead chose a simple diet and a simple lifestyle. His ability to detach from the love of the world, positioned him to clearly hear the voice of God. The prophet will lose his kingdom position if he is not truly loyal and committed to God. Jesus validated John's allegiance and his calling in **St. Matthew 11:8:** ***"But what went ye out for to see? A man clothed in soft raiment? Behold, they that wear soft clothing are in kings' houses."***

Please take great care as you carry your prophetic gift. It must not be tainted by a lack of humility, fear, or a worldly appetite. The gift must be carried in the

♦ ♦ ♦

spirit of excellence. The following "Prophet's Check List" is designed to provoke you to maintain the eternal order of your calling and, if you have lost focus, will help you to refocus.

The Prophet's Check List:

1. Is your gift influenced by people in authority or by God?

2. Do you fear what you may lose if you speak the word God has given you?

3. Are you willing to forsake your current status in a local assembly or among your family and friends?

4. Are you accountable to other prophets so that they can judge your gift without any offense?

♦   ♦   ♦

Chapter 8—How to Carry This Gift
The Office of the Prophet

5. Are you worried about being on someone's payroll rather than God's roll?

If you are challenged in any of these areas, I encourage you to stop now and repeat this powerful prayer with humility and sincerity:

> *Dear Lord Jesus, please forgive me for allowing the gift you have given me to be controlled by my selfish motives and my lack of insight.*
>
> *Forgive me for allowing men and women, and prestige and power to influence how I govern your prophetic gifting in my life. I believe that you will set me free from this bondage. I will not allow myself to become blinded*

Chapter 8—How to Carry This Gift
The Office of the Prophet

> *from your righteousness again, causing the prophetic gifting to be bound.*
>
> *I will say what you want me to say. I will do what you want me to do. I will go where you want me to go. I surrender this gift of prophecy to you and I promise to never use it with malice in my heart. I will always operate in the spirit of love as I flow in the prophetic, so help me God.*
>
> *It is in Jesus' name I pray. Amen.*

♦ ♦ ♦

Chapter 8—How to Carry This Gift
The Office of the Prophet

My Prophetic Pathway

As a young minister, I could not get enough of the word of God and read it morning and night. Sadly however, a bad spirit began to work in me; I walked into the church not only full of the word of God, but also full of myself. I portrayed myself as not wanting to say anything, but secretly I could not wait for opportunities to share. Instead of sharing testimonies that demonstrated God's goodness in my life, I preached mini-sermons under the power of God. But after a while I felt awkward and uneasy when it was time for testimony service.

The Lord revealed my problem, "You have vain humility." Boy, this statement was difficult to swallow! I thought that the Lord surely does not mean this about me. But He began to reveal the hidden secrets of my heart and that the thoughts and intents of my heart did not line up with the words that came out of my mouth. Amazed, I could only agree and say amen. He rebuked me for coming to church and telling my pastor that I did not want to preach. He said, "I have called you to preach my word and when you tell others that you have nothing to say when you really do, you are operating

---

♦ ♦ ♦

Chapter 8—How to Carry This Gift
The Office of the Prophet

> in vain humility."
>
> Thereafter, I went to Bishop Holiman admitting my vanity and that I really did have something to say for the Lord when I came to church. In his humble way, Bishop Holiman spoke to me as an apostolic father by kindly affirming that he understood. After this confession to Bishop Holiman, I began to learn what it means to walk humbly before the Lord and became a faithful servant to both my pastor and the congregation at Bethsaida Temple. The Lord taught me many things in that local house—I learned how to faithfully serve in various capacities and, from the relationships cultivated and fostered there, I learned how to carry the gift with humility and love for humanity.

Questions *(Provide scripture references where applicable)*:

1. Why is the conduct of the prophet of any consequence when dealing with and speaking to humanity?

♦ ♦ ♦

Chapter 8—How to Carry This Gift
The Office of the Prophet

2. Can you remember a time when your conduct negatively impacted your prophetic influence? If so, how did you overcome that experience?

3. How will you incorporate the words of **2 Corinthians 4:7** to ensure you will walk in prophetic excellence?

4. As you read this chapter and desire to properly carry your gift with excellence, has God convicted your heart concerning your walk with Him? If so, have you repented.

♦ ♦ ♦

Chapter 8—How to Carry This Gift
The Office of the Prophet

_____

_____

_____

_____

_____

_____

♦   ♦   ♦

THE OFFICE OF THE PROPHET

CHAPTER 9

HOW TO SERVE IN THE LOCAL HOUSE

The pastoral, the apostolic and the prophetic must work together in harmonious agreement. After acknowledging and accepting the prophetic calling, the prophet must ensure he is planted in the right house. Ideally, he should seek a house where the prophetic is both welcomed and celebrated. God has placed His prophetic voice in the local assembly to be His eyes and ears. Often, the prophet will discern things in the spirit long before the pastor or leader of the house does. The heart of the prophet must be pure and humble as it relates to leadership, so that the prophetic gift operates without interruption.

Chapter 9—How to Serve in the Local House
The Office of the Prophet

I would postulate that a "best practice" for the prophet of God serving in a local house is to avoid the undertaking of a leadership position. The politics and status of the leadership position can encumber the prophet of God and inhibit him from freely speaking the will of God in the local house.

Another "best practice" for the prophet of God is to separate himself from schisms, divisions, and special interest groups who are influential in the local house. If the prophet of God is negatively persuaded or influenced by any group, by a position, or by a title, he will be more concerned about the political environment and less concerned about working in the Kingdom of God. Furthermore, the prophet runs the risk of losing his sensitivity to the voice of God.

An atmosphere where the prophetic is not warmly welcomed and received will inevitably kill the prophetic gift. There are

Chapter 9—How to Serve in the Local House
The Office of the Prophet

leaders who only *tolerate* the prophetic, but fail to embrace and adopt God's prophetic gifting. Rarely will this type of leader acknowledge the gift or publicly endorse the prophet. The prophet will become a threat to insecure leadership and, therefore, is not allowed an opportunity to minister during corporate worship.

What causes leadership to only tolerate the prophetic gift rather than to celebrate it? The answer is secret sin. When those in leadership are practicing secret sin, they will not want the prophetic to flow because it will reveal their sin. Therefore, these leaders will do all they can to redirect the attention on human efforts and away from the divine order of Kingdom flow.

Because of the tremendous weight and authority of the prophetic gifting, it is difficult for those untrained in prophetic ministry to embrace and accept the prophetic. Both Old and New Testament

♦ ♦ ♦

Chapter 9—How to Serve in the Local House
The Office of the Prophet

prophets had one job description: to speak the oracles of God. In most cases, God required the prophets to confront sin in the camp. When unrighteousness is tolerated or celebrated in leadership, there will be great opposition to the prophetic and resentment will begin to abide in the hearts of those in the local house. Once again, the prophet of God must gird his loins and embrace his reward—the prophet will not be received in his own country or home,[147] and will be rejected from fellowship in his local house.

When celebrated in the local house, the prophetic gifting becomes very much a part of the leadership. In turn, leadership acts as the apostolic voice within the local body. Note that where there is disunity among leadership, the voice of the prophet will be instrumental in identifying and resolving issues.

---

[147] Matthew 13:57

Chapter 9—How to Serve in the Local House
The Office of the Prophet

In many instances, the prophet will see things long before the leadership recognizes there is a problem. However, this does not (and should not) cause contention in the house. If you are at the right house and are truly submitted to leadership, you will receive grace to patiently wait for God to reveal to the leadership His plan to address issues. While waiting on God's timing, the prophet must trust God and not become frustrated or anxious. How will you know if you are at the wrong house? Those in authority will not receive you in peace and they will not hear your words.[148]

As Jesus sent forth His disciples to preach the impending arrival of the kingdom of heaven, He instructed them to use a litmus test to determine when to enter a house and leave a peace blessing or when to leave and shake the dust off of their feet.

---

[148] St. Matthew 10:13

♦   ♦   ♦

Chapter 9—How to Serve in the Local House
The Office of the Prophet

The apostles are to *stay* if the family believes in Jesus. They are to *depart* if Jesus is rejected.[149] Many of God's prophets have met their spiritual demise by remaining in houses that refused to accept their peace. This has been harmful to the body of Christ and has stifled effective prophetic ministry—that body is no longer hearing the voice of God.

In Chapter 3, I mentioned the account of Obadiah in **1 Kings 18** and the effect of the spirit of Jezebel. To provide further exposition, the Jezebel spirit is neither male nor female, but it is terrified of the prophetic voice sent by God. From ancient times until the present day, Jezebel recognizes that when God's prophet shows up, her time is short and it is diminishing. When operating and serving in the right local house, the prophet is able to determine

---

[149] St. Matthew 10:9-14

the power of this spirit as he assesses how leadership embraces the prophetic—is it embraced in peace or is it rejected in hostility?

For clarification, the fact that the prophetic gift is not used in each corporate worship service is not an indication that the prophetic is rejected. Every local house needs the prophetic sound of God released at sundry times for clarity, direction, and discernment for God's people. It is for the prophet to discern whether the prophetic is received and celebrated or rejected and despised.

The enemy will work overtime to cause division among leadership, thereby hindering the prophetic. The prophet must guard against fault-finding in the house. This stronghold will begin to work in the mind of leadership to drive away the gift from the house. If the gift is driven from the house, the people are not hearing from God!

♦ ♦ ♦

Chapter 9—How to Serve in the Local House
The Office of the Prophet

If the people are not hearing from God, they are in trouble! The prophet must immediately pull down the stronghold of fault-finding.

There are no lone rangers in God's Kingdom. He has placed each member in the body "fitly," so that it may supply nourishment to the body as needed.[150] Therefore, the prophet must be aware of the symptoms that indicate a demonic attack against the prophetic. Suspicion of leadership and authority in the heart of the prophet causes the gift of discernment to be disrupted. Few today teach this important lesson about serving in the local house. Unfortunately, this lack of teaching has caused many prophets to become sad casualties.

---

[150] Ephesians 4:16

Chapter 9—How to Serve in the Local House
The Office of the Prophet

When suspicion of leadership sets up in the heart of the prophet, he becomes incapable of proper discernment. And when this occurs, he will miss it. These are all symptoms of the attack of the demonic against the prophetic. Once again, few are teaching this lesson, which is the reason many of the prophets of God in this age have become "wandering stars." They have become casualties in the heavenly battle.

Judas and Silas, prophets in the early church, did not break rank.[151] Their job was to strengthen the local assembly, but they were submitted to the apostolic headship of Paul and Barnabas. The local assembly was edified because of their submission.

The Holy Ghost uses the prophet to sanction and ordain the work of the ministry. In **Acts 13**, the prophets sent forth Paul and

---

[151] Acts 15:32-33

Chapter 9—How to Serve in the Local House
The Office of the Prophet

Barnabas,[152] under the leadership of the eleven who walked with Jesus. Always remember that your title is not as important as the operation and results of your calling. Your calling is for the perfecting of the saints and the edifying of the body of Christ. ***Until we all come in the unity of the faith and of the knowledge of the son of God into a perfect man into the measure of the stature of the fulness of Christ.*** **(Ephesians 4:13)** This goal never changes! God intends for His church to be a strong house—not a weak house. When both the apostolic and the prophetic work together in unity, this goal is accomplished. The Bible says that if we are to see the Lord, we must *[f]ollow peace with all men, and holiness*.[153] The prophet of God must continually lay before God as he submits to the authority of his local church.

---

[152] Acts 13:1-4

[153] Hebrews 12:14

Chapter 9—How to Serve in the Local House
The Office of the Prophet

> ## My Prophetic Pathway
>
> For the past two decades, God has been gracious to me in ministry. One reason I have been able to remain steadfast in kingdom work is that after returning to Bethsaida Temple, I submitted myself to the apostolic covering of Bishop Holiman. Once again, it was at Bethsaida Temple where the Lord taught me how to patiently wait upon His guidance and how to wait for His timing. Bishop Holiman is a profound Bible teacher who imparted the truths of the word of God and his teaching helped develop in me an insatiable appetite for the word of God. While there I never sought or asked for a title or position; I simply served and was 100% supportive of the vision of this apostolic leader. God helped me to avoid entanglement with schisms within the ministry and those—who can be found in any church—who desired to negatively influence my walk. The Lord opened my eyes to watch and pray for my pastor and for the success of the ministry.
>
> I began to share in confidence the revelations I received from the Lord with my apostle. I trusted Bishop Holiman to guide and train me how to handle

◆ ◆ ◆

Chapter 9—How to Serve in the Local House
The Office of the Prophet

> the words that God spoke. I also discovered that I needed the Holy Ghost to carefully guide me so that I would not bring a reproach against the church of the living God.
>
> There were some who tried in vain to turn me against leadership. Because God kindly revealed to me their motives in advance, I was able to respond appropriately. Using wisdom, I did not discuss these situations with my pastor, but confronted with the word of God, those who attempted to sow seeds of discord in my heart. This happened on more than one occasion by some who recognized the prophetic anointing on my life. Once I fully recognized my assignment to my apostolic covering, it was not difficult for me to serve in my local house. With eagerness of heart I anticipated hearing my pastor facilitate the word of God ... and thereby we grew. To this day, Bishop Holiman and I are dear friends and brothers in the Lord.

Questions *(Provide scripture references where applicable)*:

1. Although your calling is divine, why is it necessary to have apostolic

♦ ♦ ♦

validation and confirmation concerning your ministry?

2. Can you recall an experience when your prophetic operation was in disunity with your apostolic headship?

3. What is the significance of understanding the operation of your calling from a worldwide viewpoint?

4. What can the prophet of God do to promote healing when he recognizes the prophetic is not embraced in his local house?

♦ ♦ ♦

Chapter 9—How to Serve in the Local House
The Office of the Prophet

THE OFFICE OF THE PROPHET

CHAPTER 10

HOW TO SERVE IN GOVERNMENTAL AFFAIRS

The office of the prophetic is important in governmental affairs and even more vital in protecting the lives of every citizen in the world. History and experience have taught me that we should never say "never," because we do not know what life may bring our way. The prophet must always be willing to embrace God's purpose and plan, and to submit to God's destiny for his life. Despite the longstanding dispute concerning the separation of church and state, there is a place in government for the prophetic. God, who is sovereign, will have His voice heard and His will accomplished in the earth. You will see that in the Old Testament, the prophetic voice directly influenced the kings of the land in one way or the other. In fact,

Chapter 10—How to Serve in Governmental Affairs
The Office of the Prophet

when the righteous are in authority, the people rejoice.[154]

In Chapter 3 when discussing the Audience of the Prophet, we mentioned the prophetic voice being released to those who are in influential positions. There are certain cultural influences in society which are referred to as The Seven Pillars of Society: (1) family, (2) faith, (3) education, (4) government, (5) business, (6) media, and (7) the Arts & entertainment. The prophetic voice is strategically positioned within these seven pillars. God strategically positioned the Old and New Testament prophets where His voice could be heard by those influential leaders who affected these seven areas of society. Taking time to carefully study the paradigm of biblical societies will provide insight to the prophet when prophesying to our present-day leaders.

---

[154] Proverbs 29:2

♦ ♦ ♦

Chapter 10—How to Serve in Governmental Affairs
The Office of the Prophet

The influence of the spirit of antichrist operates in civil affairs. The wise and cautious prophet will never lose sight of his purpose, regardless of the evil that is encountered. Although the prophet Daniel never ran for office, he was given a charge to respond to a civil situation caused by the signing of a decree by king Nebuchadnezzar. Nebuchadnezzar had a dream that troubled him and he could not sleep. *"Then the king commanded to call the magicians, and the astrologers, and the sorcerers, and the Chaldeans, for to shew the king his dreams. So they came and stood before the king."* **(Daniel 2:2)** What he demanded from them was a human impossibility. He demanded that they not only interpret of his dream, but that they tell him exactly what he dreamed! Failure to do so would cost their lives. Nebuchadnezzar created a national crisis that presented a common crisis that would directly affect not only Daniel's life, but the lives of his

Chapter 10—How to Serve in Governmental Affairs
The Office of the Prophet

colleagues as well. Common crisis always breeds communion. In desperation, Daniel sought the true and living God to reveal to him this secret dream in order to save all of their lives.[155] God delivered—He showed up in a dream and provided revelation of the mystery Daniel needed to solve! Before answering the king, Daniel made sure that Nebuchadnezzar knew, without any doubt, that no man could do what his God can do. He made it clear to the king that there is a God in heaven who reveals secrets! After Daniel revealed to Nebuchadnezzar the dream and the interpretation thereof, the king promoted Daniel.[156] Nebuchadnezzar then blessed Daniel's God and declared that He is God above all other gods!

While the commission to serve as a prophet in civil government is difficult, it is

---

[155] Daniel 2:22

[156] Psalms 75:6

Chapter 10—How to Serve in Governmental Affairs
The Office of the Prophet

not impossible. In order for a prophet to serve his government, his "ego must go." Along with the opportunity to lead and govern in a political position is the mesmerizing allure of power and validation. The enemy will tempt the prophet by showing him what the kingdoms of the world have to offer—he even had the audacity to try to tempt Jesus.[157] We have witnessed the fall of many politicians brought down by the lure of power, fortune, and celebrity status. The moment the prophet becomes intrigued by a position, he is finished. This is a slippery slope that has entangled many.[158] The powers of darkness, which rule in high places,[159] fiercely target all who enter their domain, and who are armed with the ability to impact change with their power and influence. If your motives

---

[157] St. Matthew 4:8

[158] Jeremiah 23:12

[159] Ephesians 6:12

♦ ♦ ♦

Chapter 10—How to Serve in Governmental Affairs
The Office of the Prophet

are not pure and you are not consecrated, you will succumb to the seductiveness of this power. This is why, as he prepares for ministry to government and civil administrations, the prophet must rely solely on Jehovah as his provider. Consider Balaam[160] and Gehazi,[161] who were both called to civil leadership, and were enticed[162] by the promises of great riches. The prophet's message cannot be swayed by, or subject to the systems of this world in any way, shape, or form.

Our governments and world systems depend upon apostolic and prophetic influence—just like Elijah and Elisha were needed and were the apostolic headship of the prophets and their sons. I believe this

---

[160] Numbers 22:7

[161] 2 Kings 5:20

[162] James 1:14

Chapter 10—How to Serve in Governmental Affairs
The Office of the Prophet

teaching is lacking in the church today, but it must be taught.

Allow me to make another cautionary observation. While public and civic platforms are important and God wants the prophetic to be highly visible in these arenas, it is very difficult for a prophet of God to enter civil government without first being fully connected to the apostolic. The prophetic and the apostolic go together like bread and butter. Influence is more important than any position or any title. I would rather have godly influence than a position or a title. When the prophet of God succumbs to the seduction of wealth and the honor of men, it is because he is inebriated with pride and lust. He has become spiritually shipwrecked, just like the sons of Eli.

The United States government is divided into three branches: the Executive Branch (President and Commander-in-

♦ ♦ ♦

Chief), the Legislative Branch (House of Representatives and the Senate), and the Judicial Branch (Supreme Court and federal judiciary). Each branch is designed to hold the other branches accountable so that no one branch will gain an extraordinary amount of power. However, under our system of democracy, there has been a mass infiltration of false prophets who use money, power, and position to negatively influence our culture. They are called lobbyists, those who "attempt to influence with regard to policy decisions, and especially proposals for legislation," and they "promote to secure passage of (as legislation) by influencing public officials."[163] In other words, they "wine and dine" to induce agreement with or sway influence in their direction to promote and endorse their own agendas.

---

[163] "Lobby," *Webster's Third New International Dictionary of the English Language*, unabridged. Merriam-Webster, Inc. (1993).

Chapter 10—How to Serve in Governmental Affairs
The Office of the Prophet

While many lobbyists judiciously operate at a grassroots level defending the minority masses from governmental and social injustices, many more have unconscionably evil agendas. From a spiritual perspective, they are political whores who have sold their souls to the spirit of Jezebel. They romance and seduce those who have the power to institute laws and statutes that directly affect the seven pillars of society.

Because the desire to hear the prophetic voice of God is lacking in government, the spirit of Jezebel rampantly runs up and down the corridors of justice, voraciously influencing governmental affairs. Those with evil agendas are terrified that the prophetic voice will speak judgment against their evil agendas and they struggle to do all they can to keep their position. Therefore, when a prophet of God is commissioned by God and strategically

♦ ♦ ♦

Chapter 10—How to Serve in Governmental Affairs
The Office of the Prophet

positioned to address authority, he becomes a spiritual terrorist and threat to homeland security. The prophet must protect himself by remaining outside that evil circle of influence and must never compromise by eating and drinking at Jezebel's table.

Although our civil leaders should be accessible to all of us, many times our culture makes them appear larger than life, because of their title and position. We must remember that they are men and women, just like us. They want the same things that we want out of life, and are not exempt from life's challenges. However, many of them, deceived by the world system, truly believe that they can change society through civil means. As noble as that may seem to the world and to those who do not know God, the child of God recognizes that there is only one true King. All people are subject to, and servants of, the king they serve.[164]

---

[164] St. Luke 16:13

♦　　♦　　♦

Chapter 10—How to Serve in Governmental Affairs
The Office of the Prophet

Therefore, if you serve a political party and have become a constituent of that kingdom, you are limited to how much power and authority you can exert in that kingdom. You have become subject to the rule of that king's authority. However, the prophetic voice of God does not have a party preference. The moment a prophet becomes defined by a party, he will become lost in an agenda that is not God's. Sadly, he has limited access to the heavens.

In Chapter 3, we discussed Elijah's statement, **"There shall not be dew nor rain these years, but according to my word."**[165] Later in the narrative of **1 Kings 18**, Elijah met Obadiah, a governor in the court of King Ahab's house. When Elijah approached him and advised him of his intentions, Obadiah revealed that he was a prophet. He confessed that he was hiding

---

[165] I Kings 17:1

Chapter 10—How to Serve in Governmental Affairs
The Office of the Prophet

100 prophets in a cave—he was hiding them in the king's domain. Obadiah was hiding them from the powers of the rulers of darkness in that region, Ahab and Jezebel. Jezebel is the ruling spirit of politics (and yes, she wears a suit and tie). Obadiah traded his precious gift—prophetic influence—for civil influence, a title, and a position. Even though he was able to conceal his secret and function as a governor in the king's house, he (along with the other 100 prophets) was not effective in his prophetic gifting. When Elijah challenged Obadiah to take a message to the king, he was so afraid for his life and of losing his status and livelihood, that he was unable to readily respond to Elijah's apostolic order. Many prophets are hiding in kings' palaces. They believe that they are doing some good or looking out for other prophets. They are wrong. They have compromised their divine assignment—to influence the nations.

♦ ♦ ♦

Chapter 10—How to Serve in Governmental Affairs
The Office of the Prophet

Our civic leaders need a friend who will challenge them with truth and who will share the righteousness and full counsel of God. A wise person will seek counsel with the understanding that the decisions they make directly affect the lives of others.[166] Therefore, the prophet needs to be taught how to change the mind of the ungodly, by his influence in the earth. God's prophet must pattern his life according to Psalms 1—***he must not walk in the counsel of the ungodly, or stand in the way of sinners, or sit in the seat of the scornful***.

The influence of the prophetic must be demonstrated in every aspect of his life—in his private life and in his public life. This is God's order and it is the will of God in the earth, for every dispensation. God is immutable and He does not change.[167]

---

[166] Proverbs 20:18, Proverbs 24:6

[167] Malachi 3:6

Chapter 10—How to Serve in Governmental Affairs
The Office of the Prophet

The prophet must not use his prophetic influence for personal gain, but must always guard against the trap of selfish ambition. You do not need a position or title, or fame or fortune to fulfill God's purpose in your life. When you have a true calling, great men will seek you out.[168] Because the king's heart is in the hand of the Lord,[169] the Lord will provoke the king to seek after the prophet. Once the prophet is given an audience with the king, the prophet will not allow the king to place his finger in his eyes to blind him from his motives. The prophet will be able to see the nakedness and transparency of the king, as well as any hidden agenda. Moreover, the prophet will be able to speak directly to the king without fear of reprisal or intimidation. The Prophet Isaiah was not afraid to speak unfavorably to, or prophesy against any king. He was not

---

[168] Proverbs 18:16

[169] Proverbs 21:1

Chapter 10—How to Serve in Governmental Affairs
The Office of the Prophet

intimidated, but took the position that he would always only say whatever God told him to say.[170] He would not allow anyone to sway him.

While I have had many experiences in the prophetic too numerous to share in this book, God has not yet given me an audience in government. But He has revealed to me through His word wisdom and knowledge to understand how the prophetic has and will impact governmental systems. The prophet of God must stay free from the need to attain reputation and fame, as well as the temptation to acquire great wealth and riches. A fame-seeking prophet will ultimately degrade the gift of God, because he is easily bought. It takes only one opportunity and, in that moment, the prophet can be bribed and persuaded to compromise his gift. Beware—the cost of

---

[170] 1 Kings 22:14

Chapter 10—How to Serve in Governmental Affairs
The Office of the Prophet

compromise is costly and, in some cases, fatal. Even when addressing governments, the prophet must warn the king to uphold the righteousness of God concerning the affairs of men.

Questions *(Provide scripture references where applicable)*:

1. What are the lessons to be learned from Daniel's example as a prophet in governmental affairs?

2. Has God spoken to you concerning your prophetic influence in your local town, city, county, municipality, state, or region?

3. What are some of the temptations in government and politics that must be avoided, so that the testimony of the prophet is not compromised?

♦ ♦ ♦

Chapter 10—How to Serve in Governmental Affairs
The Office of the Prophet

4. As you assess your sphere of influence, are you influential in the lives of any political figures? If so, how has your influence made a difference?

5. Are you willing to remain an influential figure in their lives without aligning yourself to their political agenda?

♦ ♦ ♦

Chapter 10—How to Serve in Governmental Affairs
The Office of the Prophet

_____

_____

_____

_____

_____

_____

_____

♦   ♦   ♦

THE OFFICE OF THE PROPHET

♦   ♦   ♦

CHAPTER 11

HOW TO SEE INTO THE SPIRIT WORLD

It is extremely important that the prophet completely comprehends this chapter. Many Christians become spooked when this subject comes up and they lose focus on Jesus Christ. So let me say this right up front: the Bible is our roadmap. I want all that the Bible teaches. Because God is supernatural and divine, it is not necessary for us to construct teachings that are not biblically sound. When a person becomes infatuated by the supernatural, it is easy for them to be led astray. One of the most important things a prophet of God can discover is how to navigate the spirit world. Therefore, this chapter deals with the subject of discernment or "seeing into the spirit world.

♦   ♦   ♦

Chapter 11—How to See Into the Spirit World
The Office of the Prophet

Before we go further, I encourage the prophet of God to pause and faithfully consider Jesus' admonition concerning the spirit world in **Matthew 24:4**: ***Take heed that no man deceive you.***

There is a thin line between the realm of light and the realm of darkness. Through my experience in the prophetic, I have learned that the God of the Bible will reveal heaven to his servant simply as he reads the Bible and wholeheartedly believes the truths contained therein. So as we discuss this important topic, please do not begin chasing after signs and wonders. The Bible says that signs and wonders will *"follow them that believe."*[171]

When the heavens are opened up to the prophet, he is in direct communication with the spirit of the living God! In the very

---

[171] St. Mark 16:17

♦ ♦ ♦

Chapter 11—How to See Into the Spirit World
The Office of the Prophet

moment (*kairos*) the prophet acquiesces to the Spirit of God by faith, he receives the word of God. *Kairos* is a Greek expression meaning "a time when conditions are right for the accomplishment of a crucial action; the opportune and decisive moment."[172] That which is spoken in his heart (the deep reflective consciousness of man) or *kardia*,[173] is expressly delivered by God to the prophet.

Ezekiel said that when the heavens were opened to him, he saw visions of God.[174] Another term used in the Bible is an "open heaven." I compare this to a prophetic highway used by God where He first grants

---

[172] "Kairos," *Webster's Third New International Dictionary of the English Language*, unabridged. Merriam-Webster, Inc. (1993).

[173] The Greek word for heart is *kardia (*man's entire mental and moral activity both rational and emotional). Vine, W.E. *Vine's Expository Dictionary of New Testament Words*, Peabody Massachusetts (1989). Unabridged Edition.

[174] Ezekiel 1:1

access to the prophet to enter the highway. This highway, similar to Jacob's ladder,[175] transports the prophet to another dimension as he ascends and descends between heaven and earth. When this happens, the prophet of God is simultaneously granted access to an open heaven and entrance into the realm of the spirit. There he obtains immediate heavenly inspiration from the Most High God. This inspiration is the word of God revealed.

Jesus told the Pharisees that the kingdom of God does not come by observation. The kingdom of God is within[176] and cannot be seen with the natural eye. Because the prophet of God is filled with the Spirit of God, he instantly recognizes when the heavens are open and when he has entered into the realm of the

---

[175] Genesis 28:10-19

[176] St. Luke 17:20-21

Chapter 11—How to See Into the Spirit World
The Office of the Prophet

spirit. The Spirit bears witness that the prophet of God is His child. There are countless other Bible examples where God granted His prophets open heaven access.[177] Following an open heaven experience, the prophet of God has a responsibility to speak![178]

The Lord made this statement to me: "Leslie, the *why* is equally as important as the *how*." In that moment, I got it! I recognized what God wanted me to understand. It does not take a lot of discernment and biblical knowledge to figure out why the church is in the state it is in. Anyone can clearly see that most Christians say one thing, but do another. For the most part, many of today's churches are so "spooky." They have become so afraid of the supernatural power of God, that they are

---

[177] Isaiah 64:1; St. Mark 1:10; Acts 7:56, Revelation 4:1;

[178] Ezekiel 3:17

Chapter 11—How to See Into the Spirit World
The Office of the Prophet

often frightened when God shows up at their services.

The Bible is not just a book containing historical, anthropological, archeological, genealogical, and geographical facts—it is a living entity. It is the Word of the Living God! It is spirit and it is life![179] It is a book of faith for a people of faith! Christians provide a disservice to God when they read His word for informational purposes only. When Christians read God's word, they should anticipate a supernatural experience! We do not have to make things up or hype ourselves into some type of spiritual frenzy. We have every right to expect the God of the Bible to guide us into the supernatural realm.

---

[179] St. John 6:63

Chapter 11—How to See Into the Spirit World
The Office of the Prophet

While I do not want to waste a lot of time trying to build my case, here are Old and New Testament examples. Elisha prayed for his servant's eyes to be opened so he could see that God was on their side, and his eyes were opened.[180] Balaam intended to curse the children of God for personal gain, but the Lord opened his eyes and he saw the angel of the Lord standing in the way.[181] The prophet Isaiah spoke a word and the eyes of the people were closed, and they could not see.[182] Ananias laid hands on Saul (later called Paul), and his sight was restored so that he could see what it was that God wanted him to do.[183] Finally, Paul prayed for the Church at Ephesus that, ***"the eyes of your understanding being enlightened; that ye may know what is the hope of his***

---

[180] 2 Kings 6:17

[181] Numbers 22:31

[182] Isaiah 6:10

[183] Acts 9:17-18

Chapter 11—How to See Into the Spirit World
The Office of the Prophet

calling, and what the riches of the glory of his inheritance in the saints …."[184]

Now let's talk about what happens when a person becomes born again. Immediately at conversion, there is divine revelation of Jesus Christ. We cannot even call him Lord, except the Holy Ghost reveals Him to us.[185] It is the job of the Holy Ghost to guide us into all truth.[186] Nicodemus visited Jesus at night wanting to gain an academic and philosophical understanding of Jesus' revolutionary movement. But Jesus told him that he had to be born again.[187] Trust me, anyone who proclaims he is a prophet of God, but is not born again, is a false prophet. A nonbeliever or skeptic cannot see the kingdom of God because

---

[184] Ephesians 1:18

[185] 1 Corinthians 12:3

[186] St. John 16:13

[187] St. John 3:3

Chapter 11—How to See Into the Spirit World
The Office of the Prophet

seeing the kingdom of God is a right given only to lawful citizens. In Chapter 6, I told you that the prophet of God does have to become weird or strange; but he *must* be born again.

The Lord declared that in the last days, **"*I will pour out of my Spirit upon all flesh: and your sons and your daughters shall prophesy, and your young men shall see visions, and your old men shall dream dreams ....*"**[188]

Note the operative use of one of the five senses—sight—***your young men shall see visions***. Part of the prophetic package is the ability to see into the realm of the Spirit. This is a part of our inheritance! What is the key to seeing into the supernatural? Faith is the key. Paul wrote a letter to the Corinthian church and emphatically reminded them that

---

[188] Acts 2:17

Chapter 11—How to See Into the Spirit World
The Office of the Prophet

the believer walks by faith, not by sight.[189] No one takes a walk if they cannot see where they are going. A blind person cannot walk without a cane, a guide dog, or someone to lead. That is why we need the guidance of the Holy Ghost. The more we believe in the God of the Bible through faith, the more we can see into the realm of the Spirit. The prophetic gifting from God grants us this ability.

As it is in the Kingdom of God, so it is in the kingdom of darkness. The Bible speaks of divination—referred to in our modern language as clairvoyance. These mediums should not be entertained at all by Christians or by the prophet. The true prophet of God will always be distinguished by the direction of the words they speak. *The words of the true prophet lead people to* worship the God of Abraham, Isaac, and

---

[189] 2 Corinthians 5:7

Chapter 11—How to See Into the Spirit World
The Office of the Prophet

Jacob—Jesus Christ incarnate. By way of contrast, *the words of the false prophet lead people away from* the worship of God. The words of the false prophet contain cunning craft and deceit. If you ever encounter a "so-called" prophet who encourages you to believe he is the only voice, and that the Lord speaks only through him, you should run! You should run as fast as you can!

The way we can see into the realm of the spirit is by faith in the God of the Bible. Every word He has spoken is true and every promise in the Bible is available to us. We only have to believe.

Just a few more thoughts before I close this chapter. It is important to understand that the prophet's heart must be right. The heavens are closed to those who have guile, deceit, impurity, and dishonesty in their heart. Although God is merciful and extends His grace, when a prophet's heart is not right, he becomes vulnerable to and

♦ ♦ ♦

Chapter 11—How to See Into the Spirit World
The Office of the Prophet

influenced by evil spirits. It is at this point that the prophet can be fooled into thinking he is hearing and receiving a word from the Lord, when in fact, he is influenced by demons. This emphasizes that the heart of the prophet of God must be saturated and totally inundated with the truth of God's word. The prophet of God recognizes that there is nothing and there is no one else upon which he can rely upon but the spirit of the Living God.

We have discussed Gehazi and Balaam, prophets with heart issues and who struggled with covetousness. Even in the midst of their issues,[190] God continued to deal with them to accomplish His purpose. Their eyes were blinded and they needed their eyes opened. Once their eyes were opened, they were able to see what God saw. After Balaam was delivered and could see

---

[190] Numbers 24:2

clearly, he made this powerful statement in **Numbers 23:21:** *He hath not beheld iniquity in Jacob, neither hath he seen perverseness in Israel: the LORD his God is with him, and the shout of a king is among them.*

In this passage, we see how necessary it is for the prophet of God to walk in righteousness. Balaam sought the Lord several times to appease King Balak. God finally opened Balaam's eyes so that he could see into the realm of the supernatural and see what God saw. God saw no enchantment in Israel (Jacob), but there was a shout of a king in their midst. Once Balaam's heart was right before God, he was able to see clearly. We also see in this passage of scripture how God grants the prophet the ability to see in the spirit. Moreover, the prophet has the ability to curse evil when it is detected in the hearts of people. God extended his mercy to His

Chapter 11—How to See Into the Spirit World
The Office of the Prophet

people, even though they were imperfect and full of issues. However, as long as Israel walked up right before Him, God could not, and would not curse them.

There were also New Testament prophets who could see in the realm of the Spirit. Anna and Simeon saw the coming of the Messiah; God showed them that they would not die until they beheld the King of Israel.[191] Paul, in a vision, saw a man from Macedonia pleading with him to come and help.[192] On another occasion, the Lord revealed to Paul that all who remained in the boat would be spared.[193] Agabus, a true prophet of God from Jerusalem, prophesied that Paul would be betrayed by the Jews at Jerusalem and delivered to the Gentiles. He also prophesied of Paul's death.[194] The

---

[191] St. Luke 2:25-40

[192] Acts 16:9

[193] Acts 27:31

Chapter 11—How to See Into the Spirit World
The Office of the Prophet

apostle John received apocalyptic insight through the Spirit.[195]

The prophet of God cannot operate in this gift with hesitation and fear. He must exercise faith in God. The true prophet of God has his eyes open. God is able to reveal to him the deep mysteries pertaining to the Kingdom of God. God allows him to "see" new supernatural dimensions. What an honor to see into the spirit world!

> **My Prophetic Pathway**
>
> The Lord has opened the heavens and blessed me to see into the realm of the spirit many times. As a child and even before my conversion, I had unusual experiences that I did not understand then, but now understand they were experience of the spirit world—from discerning those involved in witchcraft to perceiving when close relatives would depart this

---

[194] Acts 21:10-14

[195] Revelation 1

Chapter 11—How to See Into the Spirit World
The Office of the Prophet

> life.
>
> Once an ominous spiritual entity stood in the doorway of my bedroom. Upon seeing it, I became paralyzed, but understood its purpose in coming was to afflict me in some way. Unable to speak or to move, I thought there was nothing I could do. However, I began to realize that I was simultaneously operating in two dimensions: a conscious state of being and a spiritual state of being. While I did not know what to do, my spirit man knew what to do even though I had never been taught how to operate in a spiritual dimension. I began to think on the name of Jesus, but could not open my mouth to say His name. As I struggled to say the name of Jesus, the menacing figure stood as if it dared me to withstand it. At the very moment I was able to call out the name of Jesus, the evil entity disappeared. I was thankful to wake up, open my eyes, and move my body. Many spirit-world experiences later and I would learn how to cultivate the gift of seeing into the spirit world.

◆ ◆ ◆

Chapter 11—How to See Into the Spirit World
The Office of the Prophet

Questions *(Provide scripture references where applicable)*:

1. Once given the ability to see into the spirit concerning the lives and situations of others, what is the responsibility of the prophet?

2. When you have been able to see into the spirit world, what were the spiritual and prophetic implications of that experience?

3. Now that you are able to see into the spirit world through the revelation of God, why is it important to receive instruction and mentorship from a more seasoned prophet?

4. How did Ezekiel describe what he saw when the word of the Lord came?

♦ ♦ ♦

Chapter 11—How to See Into the Spirit World
The Office of the Prophet

5. Whenever the word of the Lord came to Ezekiel, what are some of the life-changing consequences and events that impacted his life and the lives of those in his audience?

♦ ♦ ♦

Chapter 11—How to See Into the Spirit World
The Office of the Prophet

♦ ♦ ♦

THE OFFICE OF THE PROPHET

♦ ♦ ♦

CHAPTER 12

THE GIFT OF DISCERNMENT WORKING IN THE PROPHET

The discerning prophet must exercise keen judgment and develop sensitivity in dealing with the human condition. In addition, when dealing with God's people, the prophet must continue to reverence God.

The body of Christ is in desperate need of prophetic discernment. For without proper discernment demonic activity runs rampant in the church. Even in the midst of what some call a "high time in the Lord," there is a tremendous need for discernment. Whenever the manifest power and presence of God rests on His people, beware and take note of [s]atan's desire to release demonic activity. In **Job 1:6**, although uninvited, [s]atan showed up: ***Now there was a day***

Chapter 12—The Gift of Discernment Working in the Prophet
The Office of the Prophet

when the sons of God came to present themselves before the LORD, and [s]atan came also among them.

The true prophet of God must beware of the spirit of fault-finding and the spirit of condemnation. The prophet of God should only speak forth God's judgments according to the prophetic rhythms of heaven. What God thinks, the prophet thinks. What God speaks, the prophet speaks. The prophet of God must speak only what is the will of God.

Fault-finding, a spirit found in many present day churches, masquerades as the prophetic voice of God. I have already mentioned that a person does not have to be "super spiritual" to find fault in the church. But the true prophet of God brings a message from the very presence of God that provokes change in the thoughts, attitudes, and opinions of people. When the prophet of

Chapter 12—The Gift of Discernment Working in the Prophet
The Office of the Prophet

God operates from a place of pure discernment, God is able to trust him.

Discernment is critical in the life of the prophet of God. One main reason I wrote *The Office of the Prophet* is to impart foundational truths to the prophet. My prayer is that this body of work is helpful not only to young prophets, but that it also encourages and inspires God's seasoned prophets.

As the prophet receives revelation from God, he must recognize that he is literally standing in the very presence of God and in the place of God.[196] The prophet is standing before the King of Kings, the Lord of Lords, and the sovereign, righteous, and Holy God.

---

[196] 2 Kings 3:14

Chapter 12—The Gift of Discernment Working in the Prophet
The Office of the Prophet

To maximize the gifting of God in his life, the prophet must have clean hands and his heart must be pure.[197] He must be free from the soulful lusts and the vanity of the world. His mouth must never speak deceitfully.[198] The instructions in this chapter are foundational to proper discernment.

Through the anointing of God, the discerning servant of the Lord must always say only what God says.[199] He must become blind to everyone and everything—except God. The word of God speaks on this wise concerning the prophet of the Lord, ***"Who is blind, but my servant …?"*** **(Isaiah 42:19)** If his soul is entangled with the affairs of this

---

[197] Job 17:9; Psalms 24:4

[198] Psalms 24:3-4

[199] Deuteronomy 18:18; 2 Peter 1:20-21

♦ ♦ ♦

Chapter 12—The Gift of Discernment Working in the Prophet
The Office of the Prophet

life, the prophet will not operate in the pureness of his calling.

The young prophet will learn that he is able to see things long before others and, as we discussed earlier, even before his leaders. Often because of immaturity, the young prophet is unable to fully articulate and communicate what is seen in the spirit. This is another slippery slope whereby the young prophet can end up believing people are against him. [s]atan will trick him in departing from the care and covering of an apostolic headship.

Once again, there is a need for mentoring by a seasoned prophet who is able to teach the young prophet how to properly discern God's word and His instructions. One instance of this type of mentoring relationship is between Moses and Joshua (the son of Nun). As Moses came down from the mountain, and as he

♦ ♦ ♦

Chapter 12—The Gift of Discernment Working in the Prophet
The Office of the Prophet

and Joshua entered the camp, Joshua's first impression was that the sound he heard was the sound of war. Through his veteran experience as a prophet, and because of his seasoned sense of discernment, Moses taught Joshua how to properly discern the sound. This example of mentorship is seen in several scriptures. For instance, when Elisha and the young sons of the prophets were gathering food to put into the pot, one of the young prophets gathered a wild vine. The vine was poisonous and would have killed them all. When they saw death in the pot, the sons screamed out to Elisha. Elisha was able to bring healing to the food. The healing in the pot allowed them to receive a wholesome and healthy meal.[200]

There is a difference between discernment and divination. Discernment means: (1) to sense or come to know

---

[200] 2 Kings 4:38-44

♦ ♦ ♦

Chapter 12—The Gift of Discernment Working in the Prophet
The Office of the Prophet

something that is hidden or obscure; and (2) to make a distinction between good and evil.[201] Divination is the art or practice that seeks to foretell future events, or disclose hidden knowledge by the use of an augur, soothsayer, or diviner.[202] These definitions are helpful metrics for establishing a line of demarcation in discerning the true gift of prophecy. The discerning prophet has learned to listen for the prophetic rhythms of heaven and will never make a mistake about the origin of his message.

There are churches that provide secret havens for those directly under the influence of the spirit of divination. Without proper discernment, these activities go undetected. Another line of demarcation

---

[201] "Discernment," *Webster's Third New International Dictionary of the English Language*, unabridged. Merriam-Webster, Inc. (1993).

[202] "Divination," *Webster's Third New International Dictionary of the English Language*, unabridged. Merriam-Webster, Inc. (1993).

♦　♦　♦

Chapter 12—The Gift of Discernment Working in the Prophet
The Office of the Prophet

between the prophet of God and the false prophet is motive. Discover the motive and you will get to the truth. The gift of divination is as simple as a card trick or fortune-telling, where a fortune teller simply reads a person. If you live long enough, you will be able to measure up a person pretty well simply by looking at them, by taking note of the way they dress, by the way they talk, their accent and dialect, etc. This is what false prophets do in the church while masquerading as prophets of God. Divination is a form of witchcraft. Sadly, most people are unaware of the difference.

Beware! Money and fortune-telling often go together. A church cannot effectively operate without money and not every offering received is evil. However, when money becomes the main focus in a church, it should be a red flag. The gift of God cannot be purchased and is not for sale.

♦ ♦ ♦

Chapter 12—The Gift of Discernment Working in the Prophet
The Office of the Prophet

Fasting, consecration, and reverence to God are all vital in receiving proper discernment. To share the divine oracles of God with humanity, the prophet must be honest and sincere about his calling to **THE OFFICE OF THE PROPHET**.

> **My Prophetic Pathway**
>
> While discernment is one of the most lethal weapons in the realm of the prophetic, it is also the least understood. As a consequence, proper training and teaching is lacking in many churches. The Bible is clear that the gifts and callings of God are without repentance, but I soon learned that if I did not handle my gift with truth, humility and a clean spirit, my discernment would become dull.
>
> My first visit to Denver was at the invitation of a friend in the military who traveled the world. Little did I know that my journey to Denver would be a major turning point in my life. So at 20 years of age, my friend, and my new girlfriend and I traveled to Denver with great expectations of what the city would offer. I had neither traveled the world nor did

♦ ♦ ♦

Chapter 12—The Gift of Discernment Working in the Prophet
The Office of the Prophet

> I have the college education that my girlfriend had. However, although I was unaware of it, the gift of discernment was already working in me and I was able to discern the spirit of certain people who began to encircle our lives. It was not long before both my girlfriend and my friend began to believe me about the people we were allowing in our lives. I once discerned that someone we met did not mean us any good. I shared this insight with my friend, but he did not listen. Later after being ripped off, he understood and was surprised that my prior warning came to pass.
>
> I had to endure some dark days to learn the tremendous life lessons that God needed me to understand to operate the gift. But through His mercy and great love, today the gift of discernment operates fluently in my life. It was only following a tragic divorce and other life events that I sincerely began to walk in true humility. Those experiences also instilled within me compassion and love for people. I am positive that I would have chosen an easier path. But God! He delivered me from times of immense and painful testing and graciously allowed me to see into my own heart—desperately wicked and deceitful is the human heart without God. And

♦ ♦ ♦

Chapter 12—The Gift of Discernment Working in the Prophet
The Office of the Prophet

> to God be the glory because he did not give up on me. He chastened me so that I would not only discern, but discern through the eyes of humility.

Questions *(Provide scripture references where applicable)*:

1. Why is sensitivity in prophetic discernment vital to the one who receives a prophecy?

2. What character traits can degrade proper discernment by the prophet?

3. Has there been a time in your ministry when your indulgence in carnal or worldly things hindered your discernment of the will of God?

4. How do the principles in **Ephesians 4:13-16** apply to the life of the prophet?

♦   ♦   ♦

Chapter 12—The Gift of Discernment Working in the Prophet
The Office of the Prophet

5. Pride is the greatest enemy to all that God desires for us. Prophet of God, are you willing to give God total access to you heart, your mind, your body, and your soul so that He may fulfill His divine purpose in your life? Yes or No.

♦   ♦   ♦

Chapter 12—The Gift of Discernment Working in the Prophet
The Office of the Prophet

_____

_____

_____

_____

_____

_____

♦ ♦ ♦

THE OFFICE OF THE PROPHET

♦ ♦ ♦

<u>AFTERWORD TO THE PROPHET</u>

The Office of the Prophet is divinely appointed by God and whom God did predestinate, them he also called.[203] The commission to serve in the area of prophecy requires a complete understanding of all of the preceding chapters, as well as an intense desire to do the will of God.

As you accept your high calling to the prophetic, I pray that you will:

1. Prayerfully contemplate the enormous responsibility that God has placed on your life;

2. Consider the demanding sacrifices that will be required of you; and

---

[203] Romans 8:30

Afterword to the Prophet
The Office of the Prophet

3. Reflect upon your personal experiences with God in the area of prophecy.

Once you have said yes to God, you will be ready to completely surrender yourself to a place where you can accept as truth the teachings in this book.

If you are only able to recognize a few chapters as relevant to prophetic ministry, but are sure of your election, then you are not quite ready to go forth. I, therefore, challenge you to examine yourself, lay before God, and continue seeking His face. After a time of seeking God, He will renew your mind and enlighten your heart. Then you will be able to accept every truth contained in this writing.

As a prophet, you must understand that you need God's divine intervention in every area of your life. You must not lean unto your own understanding, but you must

♦ ♦ ♦

Afterword to the Prophet
The Office of the Prophet

always lean and depend upon God. Your finite and human understanding will cause you to fall into sin and erroneously speak into the lives of others what God has not instructed you to speak. The words you speak are the words of God and the effect upon the souls of men are eternal.

Understanding who your audience is and how to develop, protect, carry, and serve in your prophetic capacity is vital, and should not be taken lightly. The souls of others are depending on the prophet to be circumspect, obedient, and knowledgeable. Prophet of God, you must operate daily from a place of love and humility for God, and for the souls of man. You must recognize that God is sovereign and just.

You are blessed with the honor of being able to see into the spirit world and the gift of discernment is imparted into your life. I have obeyed God. I have shared with you God's revelation about how to walk in

♦ ♦ ♦

Afterword to the Prophet
The Office of the Prophet

integrity and uprightness of heart. I have shared with you how to be effective in **THE OFFICE OF THE PROPHET**. I have shared with you some of my personal testimony in the prophetic.

Because the Lord has given me a discipleship ministry as well as this revelation regarding ***the office of the prophet***, it is vitally important that you recognize that the book you are holding in your hands is written by the divine inspiration and revelation of God Almighty. He desires that we all walk in the full measure and stature of Christ.

Finally, I have attempted to communicate to you how necessary it is for the Body of Christ to effectively operate in the apostolic/prophetic rhythms of God and that nothing happens without a sound. Therefore, I speak forth the gifting and calling of God in your life. I pray that it be activated with the full capacity of Kingdom

♦ ♦ ♦

Afterword to the Prophet
The Office of the Prophet

authority. You have been given everything that pertains to life and godliness, according to the knowledge of Christ.[204]

> *I command you to walk in the authority of the knowledge, which you have received, without shame, guilt, doubt, and intimidation of men or of the principalities of darkness.*
>
> *I pray this in the mighty and matchless name of Jesus Christ of Nazareth, Amen.*

~

---

[204] 2 Peter 1:3

ABOUT THE AUTHOR

Apostle Leslie D. Richardson is the founding pastor of My Father's House International Christian Discipleship Center and the author of "The Office of the Prophet," published in 2012. He and his wife, Pastor Lily R. Richardson, are the vision-bearers of this awesome ministry located in Denver, Colorado.

Pastor Richardson is the third child of four children born to Deacon O.J. and Pastor Geraldine Richardson. His parents (and late grandmother) are in the ministry, making

♦   ♦   ♦

About the Author
The Office of the Prophet

Pastor Richardson a third-generation preacher of the Gospel.

Pastor Richardson is a native of Lansing, Michigan, where he received his formal education. He studied Architectural Drafting at the Lansing Community Design Center, received his biblical training under Bishop Earl O. Holiman (Pastor of Bethsaida Temple Christian Center in Denver, Colorado), and additional training at the Marilyn Hickey Bible College.

Pastor Richardson's first pastoral assignment was as acting pastor at the Original Church of God, located at 72nd Avenue in Chicago, Illinois. After commuting between Denver and Chicago for ministry for over 2½ years, the Lord led to him to plant the ministry of My Father's House in Denver. After much prayer and fasting, and counseling from his pastor and mentor, Bishop Holiman, Pastor Richardson

♦ ♦ ♦

About the Author
The Office of the Prophet

obeyed the mandate. His two sons, Leslie II and Marcus, his sister Diane, and a few others, were the initial members of My Father's House. With the call of God on his life, and nothing but the Word of God, the Lord led him to launch the ministry of My Father's House in Denver, Colorado.

Pastor Richardson began evangelizing the Denver community with his "Crying In The Wilderness" radio ministry—and the Lord added to the Church such as should be saved. Today he is still "Crying in the Wilderness" on radio, television, and on the Internet.

The Lord has given Pastor Richardson the vision to disciple God's people, a gift to unlock the mysteries contained in God's Holy Word, and an anointed, apostolic, and prophetic ministry.

♦ ♦ ♦

About the Author
The Office of the Prophet

The Richardsons are the proud parents of four beautiful children: Leslie II, Marcus, Jasmine, and Joshua. And they have four grandchildren: Leslie III, Laila, Adriel, and Mya.

♦ ♦ ♦